GERMANY
The Federal Republic

UMSCHAU VERLAG FRANKFURT ON THE MAIN

GERMANY

THE FEDERAL REPUBLIC

A CONTEMPORARY PORTRAIT

266 COLOUR PICTURES
TEXT BY ERNST JOHANN

EDITED BY THEODOR MÜLLER-ALFELD

Our Contributors of Photographs

Lothar Kaster: 32 o., 32 u., 33, 37, 38 u., 39, 40/41, 42, 47, 49, 52/53, 65, 92/93, 97, 114, 115 u., 116, 117, 120, 121, 132, 142, 145, 151, 153, 156, 182, 183, 184 185, 188, 194/195, 196, 198/199, 200, 206/207, 212, 217, 219, 222, 223, 225, 226, 227, 232, 233, 234, 236, 237, 238, 240, 241, 242/243

Ludwig Windstoßer: 18, 19, 30, 31 o., 31 u., 34, 35, 85 o., 157, 160 u., 161, 162, 163, 169, 179, 190/191, 191, 193, 208, 209, 212/213, 215, 224, 228, 229, 230, 231, 235, 239, 244, 246, 247, 248

C. L. Schmitt: 24/25, 27 u., 28/29, 44/45, 45, 48, 56, 59, 69, 74, 86, 89 o., 89 u., 102, 103, 105, 112 o., 123, 126 o., 128 u., 129, 144, 147, 159, 173, 176, 177, 178, 200/201, 204/205

Joachim Kinkelin: 13 (Klaes), 16 o. (Löbl), 20/21 (Ziegler), 87 o. (Central-Color), 88 (Löbl), 90 Mitte rechts (Herfort), 90 u. (Klaes), 91 Mitte (Klaes), 98/99 (Ziegler), 99 (Herfort), 106 o. (Löbl), 108 o. (Bohnacker), 110 o. (Löbl), 111 (Huber), 119 (Hartz), 128 o. (Schneiders), 130/131 (Schneiders), 137 (Schneiders), 148/149 (Schneiders), 155 (Herfort), 166 (Ziegler), 197 (Huber), 199 (Hartz), 220 u. (Huber)

ZEFA: 12 u. (Schneiders), 16 u. (Schlapfer), 22 o. (Sedlmayer), 26 (Puck-Kornetzki), 27 o. (Schneiders), 29 (Freytag), 36 u. rechts (Hetz), 43 o. (Puck-Kornetzki), 43 u. (Biedermann), 54/55: (Baudisch), 68/69 (Herfort), 70 (Schneiders), 80 (Abel), 82/83 (Schneiders), 87 u. (Schröter), 92 o. (Stapelberg), 92 u. (Heilmann), 112 u. (Backhaus), 133 (Schneiders), 140 (Schneiders), 154 (Schneiders), 164/165 (Schäfer), 167 (Schneiders), 180/181 (Damm)
Toni Schneiders: 50/51, 55, 62, 64, 81, 90 o., 90 Mitte links, 91 o. links, 91 o. rechts, 91 u., 124 o., 138, 139, 146, 152, 158

Gerhard Klammet: 12 o., 17, 56/57 (Klammet & Aberl), 60/61 (Klammet & Aberl), 66/67 (Klammet & Aberl), 67 (Klammet & Aberl), 71 o. (Klammet & Aberl), 106 u., 107, 122, 131, 172 (Klammet & Aberl), 174/175, 186/187 (Klammet & Aberl)

Otto Ziegler: 58, 74/75, 94/95, 100/101, 124 u., 134/135, 168, 170/171, 216 o.

Bavaria-Verlag: 22 u. (Schmachtenberger), 36 o. (Schmachtenberger), 36 u. links (Oerter), 71 u. (Hardenberg), 78, 82 (Reckling), 84 (Schmachtenberger), 115 o.

Studio Schmidt-Luchs: 108 u., 110 u., 189, 245, 248/249
Burda Bilderdienst: 250/251, 251, 252 o., 252 u.
Friedrich Bormann: 24, 109, 150 o.
Rainer Waldkirch: 38 o., 104, 204

Emil Bauer: 127, 150 u.; Wolfgang Dietze: 203; Josef Ege: 113 o.; Robert Everts: 63; Foto Feldrapp: 126 u.; Fritz Ganzhübner: 85 u., 118; Renate Gruber: 202; Karl-H. Hatlé: 85 Mitte; Alfred Hennig: 253; Robert Holder Verlag: 22 o. rechts, 82 u.; W. Th. Jansen: 50; Peter Keetman: 23; Peter Klaes: 14/15, 125; Foto Maier: 96 o., 96 u.; Werner H. Müller: 113 u.; Heinz Müller-Brunke: 136, 143; Fritz Pahlke: 10/11, 46; Pontis Photo: 72 (Sack), 73 (Sack); Rebhuhn: 79; Milan Skaryd: 220 o., 221; Gerhard Starcke: 76 u.; Daisy Steinbeck: 76 o; Foto Thömmes: 214; Franz Thorbecke: 218; Ullstein GmbH Bilderdienst: 192 (Lehnartz); Hans Wehnert: 141
Archiv Oberkochen: 160 o.;
Bayreuther Festspiele: 77 (Lauterwasser); Deutsche Bundesbahn: 216 u.;
Presse-Abteilung Daimler Benz: 211; Presse-Abteilung des Volkswagen-Werkes: 210

Graphi Production: Adrian Cornford

Translation into English: George Kirby

© 1974 Umschau Verlag Breidenstein KG · Frankfurt am Main (English Edition)
Offset lithographs: Druck- und Buchbinderei-Werkstätten May & Co., Darmstadt
Typography: Libripresse Johannes Witt KG · Kriftel/Ts.
Printing and Binding: Mohndruck Reinhard Mohn OHG · Gütersloh

ISBN 3–524–00593–4 · Printed in Germany

Table of Contents

Preface

For a number of years now one may state in all justification that the postwar period has ended. Symbolic of the justification for this assertion was the holding of the XXth Olympic Games in Munich. As the world moved in for the opening as the guest of Germany and the jubilation of the the hosts joined in with the joy of the guests into a truly Olympic festival, a new image of Germany and the Germans also moved once and for all into the consciousness of the world.

Given this new set of circumstances it is both necessary and possible to draw a portrait of the Federal Republic of Germany as it presents itself today both to its own inhabitants and to its neighbours. Anyone attempting such a task must first reflect about how the Federal Republic came into being and the circumstances under which it came into being.

On May 9, 1945 the unconditional surrender of the German Wehrmacht went into force. The doom of the Third Reich was thus sealed. Germany not only had to face the loss of its sovereignty, but it was also partitioned and divided into zones of occupation.

A quarter of a century later instead of the Greater Germany of 1938 we now have an independent Austria once more and, what is completely new, two successor states that although of the German nation and German language and a common cultural tradition are politically as far apart as the power blocs that stand behind them. Their respective foundations, both in 1949, may be traced to the conflict of the great powers among the victors that erupted immediately after the victory. The wall cutting through Berlin was to be the landmark of this split.

The lands east of the Oder-Neisse line belong neither to the one nor the other of the two German states. They have remained in the hands of the Soviet Union and Poland.

The longer the distance in time grows of the present from the two World Wars, the more their inner cohesion becomes more apparent. The Federal Republic enjoyed all advantages that were the function of avoiding the mistakes of Versailles. Admittedly, two circumstances should be added that eased the process.

First, the Germans fall in 1945 was so abysmal that they had no other choice but to lie prostrate as they were – or to change themselves down to their very depths. The great majority chose to do the latter. The first free elections were proof of it; taking place first at the community level, then at the level of the local administrative district (equivalent of a county), then state-wide, democracy this time was carefully established, moving from the bottom to the top; the political parties acted as teachers and not by the fiat of a "National Assembly" as in 1919. The Basic Law, the constitution of the Federal Republic proclaimed on May 23, 1949, by then had cut out all clauses that had made it so easy ever since 1919 for the enemies of democracy to exploit them to the detriment of the Republic, and these were replaced by better provisions.

The second circumstance that contributed to underpinning the existence of the young Federal Republic was the simple and decisive fact that it was needed as a partner. With the ratification of the Paris Treaties on May 5, 1955 the statutes of occupation were revoked and the Federal Republic obtained its unqualified sovereignty; thus empowered, it was received four days later into the North Atlantic Treaty Organization (NATO). It was also soon sought after as a trading partner. With the successful currency reform of June 20, 1948 the basic requirements for import and export were met. Beginning at the latest on that day the German national economy began to orient itself to Europe. This was an orientation that was all the more impelling because it could simultaneously proclaim Europe to be the fatherland of the future.

As the outline of this illustrated volume was being planned as "a portrait of the present day", it was felt that the blessings of the economic miracle had become such a commonplace that they no longer needed to occupy centre stage in the discussion. Thus for the first time, as it would seem, since anyone has attempted to draw a portrait of present-day German reality it was justifiably possible to omit the harsh strain of poverty. Poverty still exists in individual cases, but it is no longer a mass phenomenon. In its place this volume can emphasize more gratifying aspects of life. These are the general representative and benign consequences that are due especially to more freedom of time, a benefit of the 40-hour week and of a longer holiday period.

Accordingly, such a portrait of the country – and this most assuredly for the first time – need not concern itself concentratedly on aspects of the workaday world. Instead, more space can be given to the more pleasant aspect of private life. Have we made this seem much too nice? Much too rosy, much too optimistic? There can be no denying that we could have added a few less pleasant elements to our portrait that are also a part of our reality. We can could have cited the persistent pollution of the environment, the excessively high number of traffic deaths, crime, strikes and political demonstrations. But does Germany not share in these phenomena with every other affluent society? They are not peculiar to Germany.

One of the most basic of changes in the living habits of the individual citizen is a product of ever increasing motorization. The car, both deprecatingly and proudly is nicknamed the "mobile base" in Germany and it quite literally has taken citizens of the Federal Republic farther than ever before – also in terms of personal occupation, not to say of the entire national economy. No one forgets that the rise of the Federal Republic has lain in close conjunction with the rise of the car industry.

The mobility the car affords has been an essential contribution to the fact that people have come to know their own surroundings, their immediate home district. Statistics show that most cars in daily trips do not exceed a circumference of eighteen miles; longer drives are taken on the weekends and the longest on holiday trips. Eighteen miles – that does not appear to be very much at first blush; but what this signifies in actuality may be recognized in the fact that people in such a densely populated country as Germany can drive in a trice from the metropolis to the country or from the country into the metropolis. To reach the goal of an excursion or a swimming bath or a local festival in a nearby district takes only a moment's decision. This same 18-mile factor has rendered the old, long-standing notions about locating businesses obsolete. Large department stores no longer need be situated in the centre of town; a few miles out of town supermarkets and entire shopping centres are being built, these offering the great advantage of ample parking space. Or antique shops will be found at the end of village high streets – even bars and night clubs, previously the prerogative of the metropolis – will be located in converted village barns. People will drive on Sunday to church just as a matter of routine as the farmer will drive out to his fields. Commuter traffic is no longer in a one-way direction from the outlying districts into town, but may also be from town out to rural areas where the large factories have located or where nothing but housing centres have been built in the form of satellite towns.

The distance from one's immediate home district to farther flung surroundings is no greater than the transition from workday to weekend. This free time allows people to make longer excursions just as easily as to attend major sports events. A person can drive from Hamburg into the Lüneburg Heath, from Hanover into the Harz mountains, from the Ruhr into the Sauerland or along the romantic banks of the Rhine, from Cologne into the Eifel mountains, from Frankfurt into the hills of the Taunus, from Nuremberg into Franconia's "Little Switzerland", or from Munich to the Alps. People travel not to arrive somewhere but to enjoy something – the beauty of the landscape, an old half-timbered town, a cathedral. In this manner people can meet the past and past becomes present. For this reason the portrait we wish to present will lack neither Germany's characteristic landscapes nor panoramas of her great cities nor village scenes. All are represented in their multiplicity as befits such a richly endowed country. These illustrations have been arranged so as to start with the springtime to simulate the course of the seasons. And in following the sequence of nature the year's festivals have also been recalled, as in them the voice of Germany's traditions is heard. We should ill wish to neglect any of them, whether the major ones, like Christmas, or the minor local ones, like the fishermen's tournament.

To get to know the country means to get to love it. The next grouping of illustrations dovetails effortlessly with the first and takes the form of a survey of the monuments of art and architecture that have accumulated in Germany ever since the time of the Romans and that have withstood the storms of history. The eras of the ancient Germans and of knighthood have bequeathed their edifices, the Middle Ages its cathedrals, churches and abbeys, the Renaissance its town halls, and the Baroque period its palaces and gardens.

Baroque has been termed the style of the great period of reconstruction after the devastation and plunder of the Thirty Years' War. But no term has yet been devised to give a comprehensive label to the style used in the period of reconstruction after the Second World War. It is reflected in the bold statics that are the sum product of such new building materials as reinforced concrete, finer steel, glass and plastics. With them great high-rises have been built on German soil in the form of administration buildings, banks and insurance office blocks in the central parts of town and gigantic housing complexes on the outskirts. Both, whether office or residential, have become a familiar sight in the panoramas of the great population centres of Germany. In optical dimension such public buildings as railway stations, schools, churches and theatres are dwarfed by them, but as individual solutions and architectural achievements they are often more original.

The chapter "From the World of Work" has been purposefully closed with a reference to the world of science and resarch. There is where work on the future is being conducted – and what would a portrait of the present be if it failed to include the reailty of tomorrow?

But how will this tomorrow look for the Federal Republic? The present is furnishing us every possibility for a favourable future; for a long time Germany has taken its place in the leading group of Western industrial countries and having been accepted into the United Nations she has a seat and voice in the council of the nations. It is up to Germans of the present and those of generations to come to draw on the possibilities of the present to build for a propitious future.

Ernst Johann

The Rhythm of the Seasons

Spring Moves In

Always it is spring that leads in the unending round of the dance of the seasons. And always it ranks high in our fondest hopes. It strikes us as even more beautiful than the summer, which we call the beautiful season, even richer than the autumn with all its gifts, and even more secretive than the winter with its sense of fulfilment. But why? No other season makes us more conscious that we are creatures of creation itself. Nature, revivifying herself day by day, takes us to school as if we were children so that we too may learn to experience life anew. We are prepared for it in our hearts – at the latest from that hour on when we watch the February sun melting the snow away. Just as we become aware of this ordinary occurrence, those few moments arouse feelings of restiveness in us, no less powerfull for their muted embrace. From that point on we feel tied to the rhythm of the breath of creation – unless we are devoid of feeling. We joyously share this feeling with all awakening life, yet not quite so much that our spirits however revived may be wholly assured of the joy of life. Still, we never ever savour the "sweet habit of being" with quite such relish.

The Geroldsee, or Wagenbrüchsee, near the hamlet of Gerold along the German Alpine route, with the Karwendel range in the background

11

Ice thawing on the Staffelsee near Murnau

Cherry blossoms at Hagnau near Meersburg
on Lake Constance

The Blossoms as They Wander

Spring sets out on its journey on the Isle of Mainau, so blessed by its climate. There the blossoms never cease, or it would appear. Here a nonpareil outburst of budding sets forth and continues through the Rhine valley to celebrate its next victory in the pink-red almond blossoms along the Weinstrasse and the Bergstrasse on either side of the Rhine, often as early as March. In the Palatinate, west of the Rhine, the second Sunday in April is know as "Blossom Sunday" when the apricot, peach, cherry, apple and pear trees untold their splendours one after the other, all in a row, for blossom time is fructifying time; each and every of the fleeting summers that nurture this process to maturity must be given time. The blossoms as they wander like the flowers themselves, starting with the snowdrop, need around ten days to reach the north country around the Lüneburg Heath and Hamburg.

Trees in blossom along the Weinstrasse near Annweiler. In the background, the much-sung "trinity of castles": Trifels, Anebos and Scharfenburg, also known as "the Mint".

13

Frühling

Das holde Tal hat schon die Sonne wieder
Mit Frühlingsblüt- und Blumen angefüllt.
Die Nachtigall singt immer neue Lieder
Dem Hochgefühl, das ihr entgegenquillt.
Erfreue dich der gottverliehnen Gaben!
Froh, wie er dich erschuf, will er dich haben.

Goethe

Spring

The graceful vale again has its sun, / Abounds with
vernal flower and bloom. / The nightingale sings
songs ever new / To the bliss that wells up in her. /
Rejoice in these God-sent gifts! / He wishes thee
happy as when He created thee.

Johann Wolfgang von Goethe (1749–1832)

Spring in the region of the Lower Elbe between Hamburg and Stade

Spring on the Isle of Mainau, Lake Constance

Mountain meadow in the foothills of the Alps

The Spessart Forest in the springtime

Awakening Parklands

Progress in the form of civilization separates us from nature. This is a high price to pay. Big city people, one of every third person in Germany, have to pay the highest price, for their sole reliance on the hand of nature is swiftly narrowing down to what the weather forecast tells them on television. Wise city fathers do what they can; the parks they maintain are all the more important for city dwellers for their permitting them to experience what the weather map only hints at: the change of the seasons. There, surrounded by the life awakening before them, townsmen may also share in nature's recurring bloom.

In the Schlossgarten Park of Stuttgart

Waterworks in the hilltop park of Stuttgart's Killesberg

The Königssee (pp. 20–21)

Corpus Christi procession in Seeon by the Klostersee north of Bavaria's largest lake, the Chiemsee. The procession is headed towards a former Benedictine monastery with a Romanesque church on a small island connected by causeway and bridge to the mainland.

Above left: Low Sunday, the Sunday after Easter, known in Germany as White Sunday, is a favoured day in the Roman Catholic Church for children to take their First Communion

Above right: In the German Protestant Church the young are solemnly received into full communion with adults through the rite of Confirmation

A procession in Wallgau, south of the Walchensee

Within the Sound of Bells

Confirmation is intended to reinforce a youthful Protestant in his belief before he sets out in life. For the young Catholic faithful, First Communion signifies the beginning of partaking at the Lord's Table – memorable landmarks worthy of celebration never to be forgotten over a lifetime. Reverently received at the altar, they are met with just pride in their families. Palm Sunday and Low Sunday are feasts of quietitude. Their outer signs are told in processions of children into church and in the peal of bells. Ten days after Whitsunday the Catholics will celebrate Corpus Christi Day, or

"Our Lord's Day", as the feast is called near Lake Constance. The Body of Our Lord is commemorated, the mystery of the transformation of bread and wine. The host is carried in a gleaming gold monstrance through the streets, and they will be decked in flowers and carpeting, with sacred pictures and images. And it progresses in the splendid accompaniment of a procession. Bavarian peasants row their processions across their lakes; Cologne's rivermen hold one on the Rhine, the "Holy Cargo". Nature adorns her finest dress in jubilation.

≪ The Oker, rising on the Bruchberg near Altenau in the heart of the Upper Harz mountains, forms a delightful valley of rock and wood on its path to the northern edge of the range and has recently been dammed to form a multi-branched system of lakes.

Below: view over woods and meadows towards the Feldberg (4,898 ft.) in the southern reaches of the Black Forest

The Forest

The forest, forestlands. The connotation between the concept in the singular as opposed to the plural implies a world of difference. Forestlands will bring to mind an aspect of the economy, will imply a profit or loss, and so much for that. But the forest – that is something far removed from the balance sheet; it represents a value of an entirely different order, something irrational, indeed beyond the bounds of reason. But "the forest" is intrinsic to a German's nature; it is its ancient homestead, its very fountainhead.

"The forest" is the forest of legend. It invokes dreams and is the very stage of dreaming. Much as the poets have celebrated the consoling loneliness of the wood in song and story, the wanderer experiences it at first hand. Trails have been cut that traverse Germany from north to south, from east to west. Those who hike the the great stretches of forest in the central uplands have caused them to be declared "natural parks". There they may be found, met together for their daily outing, and not infrequently perhaps the lonely hiker, making his way along the trail through the Black Forest from Pforzheim to Lake Constance.

Yet one may be sure that such walks are not taken primarily for health's sake. This is felt to be but a benign aspect. Something else is more important: to experience nature. The more the urban sprawl threatens to envelop him, the more mechanical his workaday world becomes, the deeper a retreat to the woods is felt. The wanderer enters the "woodland cathedral" as poets have called it to become more reflective as the hours pass. His pause at the peak coincides with the sublimity of his mood. Stretching out before his view in the summertide will be the green undulations of mountains turning to blue in the distance or the silent wall of snow-laden pines in the winter. And as he countensplates the culmination of his journey, he savours what Gottfried Keller described in verse: "Drink, mine eyes, what the eyelids hold/Of the golden plentitude of earth!"

In the park of the Wilhelmshöhe overlooking Kassel

The Park in Summertime

The parks of our cities in the summmterime –
how unfairly we often treat them before holiday time! Our heads filled with anticipation of
the long trip ahead, we hurry across them,
because we have better things to do. Having
returned, we apologize for our hastiness, and
they are pleased to have our company for
what remains of the warm season. With their
long paths, meadows in which to sunbathe
during the noon break, swimming baths and
playgrounds, they do their best to conciliate
the returned traveller, who is now glad to be
in the park, whether it surrounds the town
centre like a wall or rambles lavishly through
the centre, as does Stuttgart's Schlossgarten.

Mediterranean paradise on German soil: the Isle of Mainau on the Überlingen tip of Lake Constance

In the Rose Garden of Bad Kissingen's spa park

27

Postcoach scene in the valley of the Franconian River Saale

Summertime in the Country

Industry predominates in our lives and our agrarian days have receded long into the past. Nevertheless, the amount of surface space occupied by cities, villages and settlements, plus inland waters and wasteland, amounts to only 15% of the total; land under cultivation, meadows and grazing land covers 56%, and even today the forests can claim 29% of the land – this because we cling to them as the source of that inner strength we feel is essential to our emotional well-being. And yet it is still the forest of Little Red Riding Hood, of Hansel and Gretel, of Grimm's fairy tales. We think of the forest, when plagued by the oppressive heat of the metropolis; we yearn for its refreshing coolness, even less than that of water, of the lakes. Land-locked, exept in the North, Germany is a country of forests; this explains the great internal stream of holiday-makers to the mountains, to rest up in forest country. Especially in the spas and summer resorts of the central uplands only a few hundred yards will serve to separate us from the bustle of the world, a short retreat into the wood. And half an hour later, if one only wishes, one may find oneself enveloped in quiet and solitude. The stag-beetle crawling over the sandy path, the woodpecker tapping in the distance, or hedged in a clearing the bramble flimmering in the sunlight – are these not lures enough to partake of joys so near? The joys of summer?

Haystacks on the Waxenstein near Garmisch-Partenkirchen

Summer Festivals

The radiant energy of summer festivals is kept localized; hence they are less susceptible to losing their original character through outside influence. Whether it means climbing on a billy goat in Deidesheim on Tuesday after Whitsunday or the shepherd's race staged in Markgröningen, tradition is adhered to. The community of Lambrecht has to offer a goat – "with good horns and pouch" – as a payment for pasturing rights. It is then auctioned off to the highest bidder in public on the open staircase of the town's beautiful town hall. The shepherds' race in Markgröningen harks back to a shepherd's gathering on St. Bartholomew's Day, and the highlight is when the lads and their girls race to see who can run the fastest barefoot across a stubble-field. As a prize the winning girl is presented a sheep, the young man a wether. The two winners are then crowned and have the honour of leading off the dance of the day. In Rothenburg-ob-der-Tauber, in a similar festival, only shepherds are allowed to dance. If an outsider tries to horn in, he will be thrown into the fountain, to the delight of all.

Markgröningen's shepherd festival. Left: Festive parade of sheep herds; above: shepherds' dance; below: the royal shepherd couple

31

The Dinkelsbühl children's parade held every year in July as a large popular festival and pageant to commemorate this town's ordeal in the Thirty Years' War and its rescue from being plundered by Swedish troops in 1632. The Dinkelsbühl children's band and the lansquenets and Swedish knights (at right) are the focal point of this festival.

≪The Ulm Fishermen's Tournament is one of the best-known festivals still preserved from the traditions of river fishermen. Its name derives from water tournaments – two-man contests in which the competitors try to knock each other from their boats with long poles. Often as not the fisher's girl salutes her winner from the shore.

On the Cannstatt meadow in the valley of the Neckar by Bad Cannstatt, now a borough of Stuttgart, the great traditional festival deriving its name from the river flats takes place every year.

Scenes from the prince's wedding pageant at Landshut: festive procession of banner-wavers; knight in armour; the wedding banquet

Pleasurable Heritage

In medieval times, to make up for their sixteen-hour working day, peasants, townsmen and workers – factories did not yet exist – lost no occasion to stage a celebration. The major and minor feasts of the Church kalendar served as the chief occasions; secondly, there were family events, from christenings to weddings to funerals; and thirdly, there were the usages of the guilds. In the south different excuses were seized upon than in the north, and in the west different than to the east. If anyone tried to make up a calendar of them, every day in summer would be booked, some booked twice and others many times over. Today they are a pleasant heritage of the past and the intricate pattern of German history. Who can name all of these events – from the children's parade at Dinkelbühl, to the princely wedding feasts as at Landshut, to the fishermen's tournament at Ulm, to the Bavarian coopers dances in Munich, and to the many shooting festivals such as at Neuss? They number in the hundreds, not even to mention a simple parish church feast, celebrated in the style of the district. As part and parcel of the origin of these festivals they are always accompanied with good food and plenty to drink.

The Neuss shooting festival, held every summer with riflemen participating from all over the Federal Republic

A scene all too familiar on the *Autobahn* in holiday time: a traffic jam≫

Below: Camping site by a river dammed in the Aggertal in the Bergisches Land

Time for Travelling

As dense as the network of Germany's *Autobahnen* may be, these much-lauded and much-disdained lanes of grey never seem to be quite up to the traffic they have to bear. This is only too obvious when the travel season begins. Two-thirds of all families take their car to go on holiday. While the nation's various state or *Länder* as they are known in German have agreed among themselves to stagger the dates of school long vacations so that the whole country will not set out all at the same time, domestic precautions can scarcely affect the international stream of traffic. The latter wells up almost simultaneously, chiefly in the north to south direction and south to north. Then the dreaded traffic jams occur, and far grimmer, the accidents. Any driver familiar with these hazards knows to respect them; he takes along sufficient provisions and sees that the children are kept entertained. Waiting makes for bad tempers. This is part of the price of admission to the holiday paradise. What form it will take differs from one person to another. West Germans like to travel abroad in Europe; other Europeans like to visit Germany. There, from the snow-covered Zugspitze to sea-girt Helgo-land, the whole range of model scenery is theirs to visit. As for attractions, West Germany offers anything from hot thermal springs to cool, deep caves. It carries the whole line of articles but one: the desert.

A special holiday treat: a Rhine cruise

Sailing regatta in Kiel Bay (pp. 40–41)

A holiday pony ride near the Erft, Lower Rhine

Beach at Kampen on the Isle of Sylt, North Friesland

A singular pastime: raft trip on the Isar in Bavaria

Hikers' wayside station in front of the cabin: Schleglalm hunting lodge on the Predigtstuhl near Bad Reichenhall with a view of the Reiteralpe and into the Saalachtal

Hiking in the mountains: view of the mountain trail from Nebelhorn to Luitpoldhaus near Oberstdorf, leading to the Seealpsee and into the Oytal

The Meaning of Hiking

The joys of hiking are free from the vagaries of vogue, for they are a gift of nature. They emanate from the pleasant feeling of bestirring one's body and this pleasurable sensation is enhanced by the fact that no material purpose is served. The practice of hiking is not unlike the practice of love. But it is not merely important that a hiker move foreward, it is also a matter of where he is hiking. In the city, where nature has receded, there are no hikers; there a person may take a stroll, go on the town, bustle about, but hike he may not. A hiker will always have a goal in mind, whether it is the meadows surrounding an upland wood to watch the deer pass by in the twilight, or if it is a resting place at the mountain top, to observe the descending slopes disappear into an ever deepening blue. He will rig himself for a hike into the night to experience the sun rising above the mountain tops, or set out in the early evening in time to meet the first stars above a clearing. The elusive moods of the morning are as familiar to him as the languor of a noon-time pause. Whoever seeks nature will learn to take nature in her wonted stride.

Origin of a Romantic

A hiker always has a goal, and nothing lies closer to his heart than his own home district. He can explore its narrower confines on weekend excursions, the more far-flung regions on holiday trips. He can try to make the week-long hike through the Black Forest from Pforzheim to Lake Constance, or he might follow along a river bank, say, from the Rhön out of the Fulda till the latter joins with the Werra to form the Weser, a river he can continue along by steamboat. He may ramble through the Lüneburg Heath for a day or several days, or hike along the shallows of the North Sea coast for an hour or for hours on end. But only by walking can he truly gain a feeling of intimacy with the land; he literally has to go meet the land. And the land in turn leisurely has prepared everything for him. It will not race by the hiker as it does with the train or the car, nor shrink to miniature proportions as seen from an airplane. Any traveller knows of the charm of a stretch of scenery, but to feel and enjoy this charm to the fullest is granted only to him on foot. Immersed in the aspect of the singular play of mountain and valley or of wind and wave, he forgets everyday cares. The beauties of his homeland make every German a romantic at heart.

The Riessersee, showing the Waxenstein and Alpspitze in the distance

View of Füssen in Bavaria with its castle, located on the left bank of the River Lech, which emerges here from the Alps into the foothills and has been dammed some six miles below the town to form the Forggensee

Boating excursion on the Tegernsee. In the background the health resort of Rottach-Egern and the Wallberg (5,649 ft.).

The Walchensee, with its surface of over six square miles and depth of over 650 feet, is the largest and deepest mountain lake on German soil. Part of its water flows from the Isar. In contrast to most other Bavarian lakes it is located in the mountains direct and is surrounded by the Walchensee mountains to the north and the chain of the Karwendel and Wetterstein ranges to the south.

What is a romantic? A dreamer who knows not what to do with the riot of his emotions? That may have been true in days gone by. But these days we reserve this concept for one who senses things more profoundly than is common. Since the beauty of the landscape speaks for itself, a rush of emotions is thought inappropriate, but by no means a deep feeling for this beauty.

A person dwelling in a distinctive landscape will reflect it in his outer appearance; it will show in his face. Before the internal migration began within Germany following the Second World War, one could speak of the "hereditary face" of the many German strains; one's descent was equated with the appearance of his ancestral home. Today these faces stamped by nature are only to be found where one's occupation demands daily concourse with nature, as with the farmer, the forester, the fisherman. Even today one can tell by looking at a face whether the person is of southern, central or northern German descent. It will pose no difficulty for the observer of the lands and regions to imagine what human faces properly belong where. They are called characteristic, because their looks fit their calling or their native region. But this is not the romantic speaking; it is the realistic observer. The brow of the romantics is not furrowed by wind and weather, only their souls.

Garden café in the harbour of Lindau on Lake Constance

Wasserburg, a much-visited site on a peninsula on the south-east tip of Lake Constance

A sense of the past resides in every romantic's soul. Before one asks oneself what is happening within oneself should he visit the Pfahldorf in Unteruhldingen on Lake Constance; one should rightfully understand that such restorations are the product of the romantic spirit. Without this spirit Cologne Cathedral would never have been completed, nor Unteruhldingen even begun. The writer Friedrich Theodor Vischer provided the literary impulse for it when he worked a Pfahldorf story into his novel *Another One,* published in 1879. It lacked scholarly exactitude; instead, it was romantic. In it he enjoins:

"Let no one wrinkle his nose
At our dwelling between moor and swamp,
Between the reed and stump of meadow
Down by the waters . . ."

The intimations of times primeval reach far into the soul of the romantic.

The pile-house replicas at Unteruhldingen on the Überlingen inlet of Lake Constance

The Benedictine Abbey of Weltenburg, located up the Danube from Kelheim, incorporates a church built by the brothers Asam; it is considered one of the major achievements of the South German Baroque.

Essing-on-the-Altmühl, dominated by ruins of Randeck Castle

Wasserburg, situated on a loop of the lower portion of the River Inn, offers a truly picturesque illustration of the gaiety of South German Baroque.

The old episcopal see of Passau is famed for its remarkable setting at the confluence of three rivers; here the Rivers Inn (left) and Ilz (right) flow into the Danube close on the German-Austrian border (picture courtesy of government of Upper Bavaria, No. G 43/1140).

The Rachelsee in the Bavarian Forest at the foot of the Gross-Rachel (4,764 ft, p. 58)

A mill in the Black Forest: Hexenloch Mill in the Wildgutachtal (p. 59)

Who is a romantic? Heinrich von Kleist, who composed *Käthchen von Heilbronn,* the most "romantic" of all German plays, most certainly was one. In one of his letters from Würzburg he describes the town. Here we find the sensibility of the romantic expressed in pristine form: "Now when I stand on the stone bridge across the River Main, separating citadel from town, and as I contemplate the flowing river that streams past mountains and meadows in a thousand bends and runs beneath my feet, it is a though I were standing longer than a lifetime filled with exultation. That is why of an evening I like to stand on this archway and let the rustle of water and air brush past. Or I turn around and follow the course of the river till it strays lost into the mountains and I stray lost into my silent revery . . . The town, I noted, lies in a basin, as if in the midst of an ampitheatre. The terraces of the surrounding mountains served in lieu of the loges. Creatures of every description peered down as spectators swelled with joy and they sang and told of their pleasure, as if in heaven's loge stood God. And from the vault of this grand theatre the crowning beams of the sun sank down and hid themselves behind the earth – for there was to be an evening performance. A blue veil enveloped the whole locality and it seemed as though the azure heaven itself had descended upon the earth. The houses in the basin huddle in dark masses like a snail's shell, and the peaks of the towers rage high into the nocturnal air like its feelers; and the ringing of the bells sounded like the hoarse call of home – and behind this the sun died out, though glowing in bright red with the rapture of a hero, and the pale light of the zodiac glimmered around it, as the head of a saint in glory."

Panorama of Würzburg, showing Marienberg Castle in the foreground (air-photo courtesy government of Upper Bavaria, No. 6 43/423)

Bordered by vineyards, the Neckar is seen near Kirchheim

Heidelberg, archetype of a romantic German city, is situated at the point at which the Neckar, flanked by the Heiligenberg and the Königstuhl mountains of the Oder wald range, emerges into the lowlands of the Rhine. It is crowned by the rambling setting of the castle, for almost five centuries the seat of the mighty Electors of the Palatinate before it was set aflame by French troops in 1689.

Heidelberg, lying where the Neckar abandons its pleasing mountains and flows into the carefully tended gardens of the fertile lowlands of the Rhine, with the red sandstone bridge that crosses it and the red sandstone castle halfway up the mountainside, formed one of earth's romantic spots before the term "romantic" was even thought of. Goethe pronounced the view from the bridge "an ideal scene", by which he meant classic, because it was there that nature had put together all components, had warranted the perfection of their internal harmony. Yet even in Goethe's lifetime this sense of harmony he felt came to be rejected. In its place came a feeling for disharmony, disjointedness, for the incomplete, for the mythical. Goethe's daytime vision was turned into a harsh nocturnal view by the "romantics" as the brothers Schlegel, their friend Arnim and the Brentanos, brother and sisters, were called. And since they centred around Heidelberg, mountains and flatlands, town and bridge slipped from their range of notice while the hill with its castle ruins became the focus of their attention. For these ruins afforded them all elements they needed as the stuff of their feelings. From the bubbling fountain in the castle's courtyard they took their view of the decaying facades – by moonlight if possible – and with them intimations of bygone glories of the nation's past. They paused not bother that this was but the provincial glory of a minor principality. And just as an industry chooses its location to satisfy its need for wood or coal or stone, intellectual movements choose their location. For German romanticism it has been Heidelberg, because there nature and art, beauty and feeling complement one another in closest proximity.

The Rhine

The Rhine is not only endowed with its beauties, but also serves a purpose. Simply stated, this consists of transporting waters melting from the Alpine snow and the Central German Uplands to the North Sea. Down as far as Mainz it performs its task admirably; with a bed of more than seven hundred yards' width it drains more than seven hundred cubic yards per second. One may best gain an idea of this magnitude if one will but imagine that this would appear as the same volume shown for a metropolitan waterworks, taken only for one single day.

The Rhine also carries out its function extremely well between Mainz and Bingen. Then, after moving around its famous knee, after following the line of least resistance in the flatland, it next transforms itself at mid-point on its course into one of the most beautiful landscapes in the world, the *Rheingau.* In sculpting this masterpiece of scenic splendour the river had once precipitously run into difficulties. Arriving at Bingen it was suddenly confronted with the imponderable impedance to travel of a traverse mountain range of slate. Choosing as ever the line of least resistance, it tried to by-pass these dark mountains and head for the bright fields of the regions around Bad Kreuznach to the south of Bingen. And there it arrived. But this tempting district turned out to be the receding roof of another stretch of mountains. And if the lake did not care to convert this landscape in perpetuity into a lake it had just formed in all pride – which is to say, to destroy it, then all would have been in vain; it had surmount the slate mountains that lay ahead by penetrating them. Fortunately this occurred in pre-historic times. The river could take its time – as much as it wished, for in truth of the matter no such thing as time yet existed. And to set forth on penetrating through these mountains the river first allowed all the waters of thawing snow accumulated from hundreds, from hundreds of thousands of years – it had plenty of time – to converge into a gigantic dammed-up lake.

Then the *Rheingau,* the dark mountains ahead, subsided for a brief while in geological time. At the point where the water level of the new lake had attained the height of the highest of these mountains of slate, the laborious task of penetration began. The river seeped across the top, and, as we know, constant drippage of water will carve through stone, especially through slate formations. That this was the case in proved by the appearance of the Rhine slopes, markings which are discernible even today at all levels of this mountain barrier of slate. Ultimately on some day in pre-historical times the river had done with this most difficult route of passage and attained as far as Coblenz; the lake dammed up anterior to Bingen could drain its downward course, and the rest – the pathway towards Holland – was a mere bagatelle.

What the river could not accomplish in its own bed – that was achieved by the inhabitants of its banks, right and left, throughout their history as far back as we can trace it. They built their habitations and castles, their churches and monasteries, launched ferries, light-weight boats and heavy barges – in short, created everything pertaining to the amenities of a community fit for human dwelling. And the vineyards – these are a legend unto themselves.

St. Goar on the Rhine with the ruins of Rheinfels Castle

The Pfalz on an island in the Rhine at Kaub, beneath Gutenfels Castle

Where Moselles Are Grown . . .

Not only did the Rhine have its difficulties in carving out its valley through the mountainous barrier confronting it between Mainz und Coblenz. The waters to the right – the Lahn – and to the left – the Moselle – wanted to flow in direct line to the Rhine. Once they had found their most expeditious route, their paths on either side followed the most beautiful meanderings imaginable – the Lahn valley with its gentle, wide-ranging curves and the Mosel with its serpentine narrows. As for the Moselle, the Romans early on picked out the many hills along the banks destined thenceforth to serve as vineyards. They number 130 astride the Moselle alone, quite apart from the many along its tributaries, the Sauer, the Saar, the Ruwer, Drohn and Lieser. Connoisseurs can distinguish whether their Moselle was cultivated on greywacke slate or on the grey-blue schist of the Hunsrück hills. The slate drinks up the sun, the precipitous terraces augment this power, and the reflection of the water reinforces this singular combined effect, fostered by the protective height of the embracing hills. How far to the north this wine-growing district lies is revealed by the sober terrain of the Hunsrück and Eifel mountains, into which the sun-favoured Moselle was able to intrude.

Cochem, one of the most splendid scenes in the Moselle valley, with its castle of the same name; destroyed by the French in 1689, it was restored in 1869–1877 (air-photo courtesy government of Upper Bavaria, No. G 43/964)

The crater lake of Schalkenmehren, one of the circular lakes in the Eifel range that bear witness to earlier volcanic activity, and especially in evidence in the vicinity of Daun and Manderscheid. Background: the Winfeld crater lake, also known as the "Crater Lake of the dead" (air photo courtesy government of Upper Bavaria, No. G 43/680)

Epic Landscapes

The sweeps of North Germany share the openness of the flatlands and the breadth of the heavens in common, the grand tract of silence. In their contrast to the drama of the mountain country, one might term them epic landscapes, for they have stories to tell – yet each has a different story than the other. There is the tranquil story of the windmill country, the sombre tale of the moor, the legendary of the avenues of birch, the vigorous lore of the dikes, the ominous of the heaths. And each of these landscapes is illuminated by a different light, covered by a different shade of green, inhabited and made inhabitable by a different breed of men. These stretches of North Germany are meant for farmers and fishermen, not for cities and industry; they are withdrawn and not companionable.

The "Ground of the Dead" near Wilsede in the Lüneburg Heath; clusters of juniper and heather are seen in this untouched dell.

Windmill in Ostgrossefehn on the Grossefehn Canal

The Island World off the North Sea Coast

Where the Federal Republic takes its share of the North Sea coast, the littoral is divided and patchy. Not only is it interrupted by the mouths of the Rivers Ems, Weser and Elbe, but anterior to it are lined the East and North Frisian Islands; river mouths and islands increase the mileage of the shoreline geometrically. The piracy of the sea, the result of its never ceasing, insatiable erosion of the coastlands, is accepted in kind and dikes are built to spite it, works of man, that give way at least once in the space of a century if we do not neglect to recall the floods. The sea has disjoined the originally continous spit of land off the shore into the islands of Borkum, Juist, Norderney, Baltrum, Langeoog, Spiekeroog and Wangerooge – to name only the largest – and has chopped those of North Friesland off from the mainland in Amrum, Föhr and Sylt – again to cite only the major islands. Between the two chains, guarding the mouths of the Elbe, Weser and Eider, the Isle of Helgoland juts up into the sea, the sole rock island in the North Sea. So many island names, so much content and so many memories from the islands – from hearing the cry of the sea gulls on the crossing, from the thrill of sunning and bathing in the nude, to the last stroll down the beach to pick up a mussel shell or a tern's feather and take it home as a reminiscence.

Left: Estuary of the Schlei emptying into the Baltic near Kappeln

Above: Beach at Juist, a townlet on an island of the same name in the East Frisian chain anterior to the German coast of the North Sea (air-photo courtesy government of Upper Bavaria, No. G 43/588)

≪ The Wilster marsh at the Lower Elbe is one of the three great fertile marshlands of this river. It is so low that like many areas of North Germany near rivers or the sea it has to be shielded from flooding and heavy tides by rugged dikes.

Land Reclamation on the North Sea Coast

The sea takes and gives. The most valuable thing its insatiable, ravenous floods robs us of is land. Only a few centuries ago the sea could wash away precious coastlands with every flood all but completely unimpededly, hundreds of square miles all told. But since then the inhabitants of the coastline are better informed than were their forefathers on how to live with the sea. They build dikes – not an enterprise for one or a few persons but for an entire community. These costly structures have to be financed and constantly maintained. But the sea also gives and one of its most useful gifts is slime – the mud and slime that build up so that the floor of the sea in coastal waters in steadily rising and this natural process is put to good use at the coast. Series of pilings are driven, with brushwood and rock filling in the intervals and are extended vertical to the dikes at distances of over 200 yards into the shallows. Ditches are dug in the space in between by means of which the water can drain away quickly and the bottom of the shallows may easily dry up. As soon as the mud ridges between the drainage trenches have built up to the vicinity of the median high-water mark by accumulating more and more slime, nature again steps in to help, because then the halophytes begin to spread, especially glasswort, and these plants make the ground firmer and cling on to the slime. Other halophytes follow after the glasswort and after a number of years a full cover of vegetation has come into being that will form valuable grazing land. But this reclaimed land is still subject to flooding and only after it has been set off by dikes will it be free from the onslaught ot the sea. Major centres of land reclamation in North Friesland at present are at the mouth of the Eider, at the northwest corner of the Eiderstedt peninsula, in the coastal regions of the Halligens and by the Hindenburgdamm, a causeway connecting the Isle of Sylt with the mainland.

Land reclamation on the North Sea:
the Eiderstedt peninsula

Langeness, one of the Halligens anterior to the North Sea coast of Schleswig-Holstein and part of the islands of North Friesland

Helgoland, Germany's lone rock bastion in the North Sea

Festival Time

So many festivals; so many excuses for them. – The pious vow of Oberammergau to be "spared from the plague"; the ambitiousness of Richard Wagner who wished to perform his "synthesis of the arts", more simply, his operas, at one single place in the world – at Bayreuth; the adventitious origins of the Recklinghausen festival; and the dozen or so places, the very settings of which demand theatrical performances. Among them are the abbey ruins at Hersfeld, the open staircase of St. Michael's at Schwäbisch-Hall, or the Luisenburg in the Fichtel mountains. They all share the summer season in common – even if some have neglected to take precautions against bad weather. There is a total of upwards of a hundred open-air theatres in West Germany. Many of them offer classical fare: Shakespeare, Goldoni, Goethe, Schiller, or Kleist and perform their works in alteration with those of modern playwrights: Shaw, Brecht or Sartre. In contrast to the boxed-in conventional stage, the open-air theatre can stage such grandiose scenes say, a man with horse and carriage – that never fail to whet the spectators' fancy. The theatre can extend to include revues. In

Festival at Bad Hersfeld: Sophocles' *Antigone* as dramatized by the poet Hölderlin; the late William Dieterle was producer in 1962; director was Pelos Katsellis.

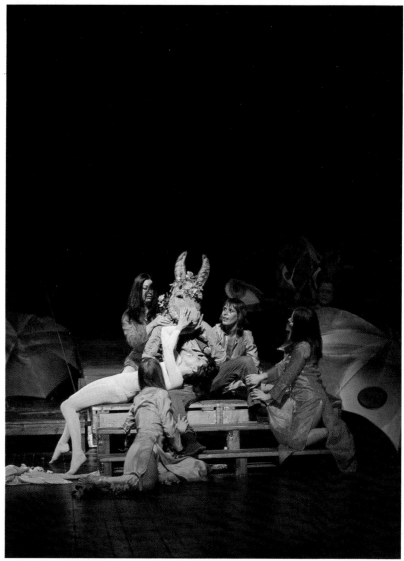

Jagsthausen the unique opportunity is afforded of experiencing Goethe's *Götz von Berlichingen* in the inner courtyard of the famed knight's own castle, with the original backdrop for its staging. Other open-air theatres harbour few literary ambitions; they content themselves with a forthright presentation of events of local historical significance, or, as in Bad Segeberg, they may be motivated by the likes of Karl May, who wrote tales of the American West. There, or in Elspe in the southern Sauerland, with its passion for Westerns, a mere horse on stage simply will not suffice; in the Indian battle the cast even throngs off the stage.

Richard Wagner Festival at Bayreuth: Act III of *Walküre* in a 1972 performance; staged and directed by Wolfgang Wagner; conductor: Horst Stein; with James King as Siegmund, Karl Ridderbusch as Hunding, Thomas Stewart as Wotan, Gwyneth Jones as Sieglinde, Catarina Ligendza as Brünnhilde, Anna Reynolds as Fricka≫

The Story of Recklinghausen

In the harsh winter of the arduous year of 1946 several members of the Hamburg stage set out on a tour of the provinces as it was usual at the time. They travelled to the Ruhr District – not to satisfy their egos, and in those days of barter exchange they had nothing to barter with. They desperately needed coal, not merely because the opera house and theatre would otherwise have to be kept closed – and this in a time when the war's survivors greeted every new performance as though it were a revelation – but also because the most valuable part of the stage equipment, the hydraulic mechanism, would otherwise break down under the cold. After talking to the managers of the coal mine "King Ludwig 4/5" at Recklinghausen-Suderwich, the Hamburg troupers did not go unheeded; they got the help they needed. It had to be behind the backs of the British Occupation authorities, who durst not learn of it. As a token of gratitude the Hamburg actors returned in May 1947 with three ensembles totalling 150 players to act for the miners of "King Ludwig 4/5". It dawned on them that they indeed had something to barter for: art for coal, and they supplied *The Marriage of*

≪The Ruhr Festival at Recklinghausen: scene from Shakespeare's *Midsummer Night's Dream* staged in 1972 by Gustav Rudolf Sellner, with Gisela Stein as Titania (centre), Werner Rundshagen as Bottom (changed to an ass), Christl Foertsch as Mustardseed, Daniela Ziegler as Peaseblossom, Ingrid Birkholz as Cobweb and Petra Ulich as Moth.

Figaro and *Don Pasquale,* plus an evening of Russian comedy, Chekhov and Tolstoy and Harward's *Das verschlossene Haus.* Inspired by this unexpected success the performances enjoyed in the heart of a workers' district, Hamburg's Presiding Mayor Brauer made the proposal of letting this barter transaction of "art for coal" become a fixed institution. A year later the German Federation of Trades Unions together with the town of Recklinghausen founded a "Society for the conduct of the Ruhr Festival". In 1950 the programme was enlarged to include art exhibitions and "European discussions". In 1957 the German Foreign Office subvented the staging of Goethe's *Iphigenie auf Tauris* and had it tour in Austria, Denmark, Norway, Sweden, Finland, France, Luxembourg, Belgium and The Netherlands. By 1965 the Ruhr Festival had occupied its own building. Five years previous, Theodor Heuss, President of the Federal Republic of Germany, had broken the ground for it: ". . . May this house be a home for the Muses, a place for human contact, a citadel of free existence." Today a summer's theatre is unthinkable without the Ruhr Festival.

◄The Oberammergau Passion Play, held every ten years. It has its origin in a vow taken by the community during the plague of 1633 and the first performance was held as early as 1634. The theatre as it appears today dates from 1930 when the previous building was extensively remodelled and expanded; the covered section for the audience contains 5200 seats.

Karl May Festival in Bad Segeberg: scene from *Beneath Vultures – Son of the Bear Hunter*. The setting is the open-air theatre on the Kalkberg, where all Karl May plays have been held since 1952.

Preparations for Farewells

The year attends to its preparations. The bustle of departure overshadows the autumn. We well know what this will lead to, but we let ourselves be pleasantly deceived: from the luminous colours of the forest that are pastels of farewell, from the pure light of clear blue skies that will soon be overcast by the white of fog, or from the pleasant warmth of water that tomorrow will turn to ice. Nature lavishes of itself and for good cause; her creatures must take a heed. Many of them, like the swallows, will be leaving us; others, like the squirrels, lay in stores; still others dig in to hibernate, for barren times lie ahead. Man understands this too, but he seems to be the last to heed the warnings of autumn. As with the passing year, yet less perceptibly, the preparations for taking farewell from the "sweet habit of being" affect his life as well.

Beech forest in the autumn

Ambience of autumn as seen in the Bärental near the Titisee in the Black Forest

Driving cattle from an Alpine pasture in Upper Bavaria

Harvest festival altar in the parish church of Wittlingen-near-Urach in the Swabian Jura

≪Wine Harvest by the River Main

Below: Wine festival in Emmingen-ab-Egg; group in Swabian peasant costume

Wine-tasting in a Swabian wine cellar

A cheerful round in the wine cellar

The Gifts of Autumn

The gifts autumn brings inspire thankfulness. Since these are gifts of nature, the fruits of the field that are harvested and stored, it is in the country where this spirit of gratitude is least neglected. It is no coincidence that the harvest festival is celebrated in the village church only after the fields have been reaped. This does not exclude celebrating the grain harvest for grain alone in places where it is the major crop. City people are usually reminded of a day of thanksgiving by an altar decked out with a few local crops. Munich's *Oktoberfest* also happens along during the time for thanksgiving. It arose out of a horse race as a part of an agricultural exhibition held an October 12, 1810, the wedding day of Bavaria's future King Ludwig I and the Princess Therese of Saxony-Hildburghausen. The memory of this day persisted and as time went by the character of this festival so loved by the Bavarians from the very start underwent changes. From a farmers' gathering, including cattle judging, it grew to be a major shooting festival. Today it lacks no popular amusement. And the quantities of beer mugs that are emptied, of roasted chicken eaten, even of oxen roasted on a spit is surpassed from one year to the next.

Festive brewery cart at Munich's *Oktoberfest*

86

View of the *Theresienwiese*, site of Munich's *Oktoberfest*

Festival in local costume in the Allgäu

Peasant costume in Upper Bavaria

Festive wagons for St. Leonhardt's Ride in Bad Tölz
(above and at right)

The Many Forms of German Farmhouses

In the beginning was the farm, the self-contained farmstead – if we do not care to go too far back and start with the caves in describing human dwelling places. Over the course of the centuries the demands of purpose together with those of climate led to the knowledge and experience that expressed itself in the structure – let us avoid the term architecture – of every farmstead. And what strikes us as an ingenious adaptation to the surrounding landscape, as say in the farmers'

cottages in North Friesland or in the Black Forest, is nothing more than subordination and arrangement to circumstance, an insigh into the immutability of the laws of sowing and reaping, of birth and transition. No farmer ever built in defiance of this underlying rationality. When necessary, he lives under the same roof with his cattle and provender; where not, he built stalls and barns separate from his family's house. The building material he had to work from was wood, but he only used this the framework in half-timbered structures filled in with a mixture of clay and straw. Ornamentation is

Above: farmhouse on the Ramsau near Berchtesgaden
Left centre: the Jodlerhof near Bayrischzell
Right centre: A Black Forest farmhouse in Aeule near the Schluchsee
Below: Half-timbered house in Verden-on-the-Aller

sparse because it would be redundant; for the simple effects the dark wooden beams make against the bright walls of clay need no further adornment. The roofs are covered with thatch or shingles; the tile roofs of the town are long held in disdain. As with the isolated farmstead, the village – a cluster of farming settlements – nestles itself into the landscape and it too seems to have grown and intertwined itself with its surroundings. Instead of building to a hundred rules and regulations, they followed only one: reason born of pragmatism.

Above left: farmhouse in Klünberg-Osterfeine near Damme in Oldenburg; above right: farmhouse on the geest at Lintig near Bederkesa; adjacent: Haubarg in Tating, dating from 1795, district of Eiderstedt

91

Wheat field on the wings of the Ruhr industrial district

Mechanized egg production

Modern milking equipment

Modern Agriculture

As agriculture dismounted from its horse and turned to the motor, it could still harbour
the thought that it would not be long before it should climb off its high horse of being an
absolute essential to the nation. In the meanwhile it has had to revise this opinion. True,
Germany no longer has to depend on its own agriculture to avoid starving while the European Common Market has made the autarchic position of agriculture obsolete. Dispelled
of the old "Blood and Soil" myth, the nation's agriculture has had to keep in step with the
world-wide demands of efficiency. The Land Reform Act of 1953 prepared the way.
Because of its traditions of inheritance south-west Germany's arable land was divided into
the tiniest strips of all, nicknamed "handkerchiefs". Acreage was so split up that one
farmer might have to have to plant his crops over a dozen or so tiny plots; efficiency was
out of the question. Then farmlands were consolidated – no easy process if one considers
how the quality of land could vary around any one village. Today this land reform has been
all but concluded. One upshot of this has been the appearance of isolated farms, where
the farmer lives in the middle of his acreage rather than in the village. Now he can put the
motor to good use; his lands are now large enough to make farm machinery profitable.
But this is only part of the story; agriculture has embarked on the next stage of becoming
more efficient; it is specializing. The crops are planted that the market demands, and
produce is geared to the optimum type of soil and climate. The farmer no longer attempts
to supply the food his family requires by himself or even for the nation at large. He is like
the factory owner manufacturing one product – in his case, chickens or wheat – and he
buys what he no longer produces himself – butter or potatoes. And this specialization
is spreading all over Europe.

Winter Charm

The first snowfall, moving in without a sound, foretells of winter's silent beauties. Snow is part and parcel of a German winter. As long as it remains on the ground it cloaks the land in white that is as gracious as it is useful; only in the towns and cities does it have a mere brief stay, for there it is regarded as a nuiusance to traffic. Children love the snowfall and even adults may catch themselves reaching their hands down to form a snowball. But this is a mere happy portent of hikes through the snow of the open field or through the forest, where only the tracks of the fleeting hare are imprinted on the virgin mantel, where the hoarfrost magically fills out the barren branches of the trees, and where fir and spruce sigh with pleasure under the weight of their white burden, the assurance of fresh beauty.

Winter charm as seen in the Black Forest (p. 94/95)

Left and below: Winter scene: Grosser Arber, Bavarian Forest

View of snow-covered Brocken (3745 ft.) in the Harz mountains

Cable-car from the Schneefernerhaus to the summit station on the Zugspitze

Münchner Haus and weather station on the west summit of the Zugspitze

The Attraction of the Zugspitze

Among the remarkable features of the Zugspitze is that it has two peaks, divided by a ridge, and at 9,738 feet is the highest mountain in Germany. It is not so much as 10,000 feet – small fry indeed when one considers that its elevation in the midst of mountains of 10,000 to 15,000 feet is comparatively modest. But that is another special thing about it. The mountain looks precipitously down on the waters of the Eibsee partway up its slope from a distance of 6,500 feet; and that is what is so imposing as it should be: from the Eibsee one may look up at over a mile of the rugged cliff of an alp. But since from below at the Eibsee the top of the mountain looks so inaccessible, to reach to insuperable summit was seen as a challenge. This obsessive wish of tens of thousands of strivers for the summit was accommodated by rail and cable car – one of the latter up from the Tyrolean side, and another with large carriages which since 1962 has ascended from the Eibsee up a length of some 17,500 feet to immediately below the peak of the mountain, as well as the Bavarian Zugspitze Railway which climbs the mountain on tracks and cog wheels. One boards it in Garmisch and its destination is the ski-lodge and hotel known as the *Schnee-fernerhaus* on the northern edge of the plateau at the top at an altitude of just over 8,704 feet. On this plateau, a broad rocky syncline between the two peaks of the Zugspitze, partly filled in by a glacier from the Schneeferner side, the highest ski run in Germany is found, a veritable paradise for ski buffs, because one may ski on it practically the whole year round. The beauties one beholds on the ride on the funicular up the Zugspitze, ever changing and wider reaching the higher one goes, prepare the traveller for the great joys he may expect at the top, reached by a short leg by cable car from the train terminus. One takes in stride the fact that, amid the splendid scenery beneath a clear blue sky, the humdrum business of a restaurant and the sale of beer, sausage and sun-tan cream goes merrily on, but pales to nothing against the ineffable majesty of the mountains.

Feeding Game in the Winter

One may participate in feeding the wild game animals as an on-looker, much as one hears the rutting-call of the deer in the woods of the Harz. Our indiscretion shies form nothing. We tap nature chummingly on the shoulder and justify our intrusion by claiming to "tend" the forest and "look after" the wild game. Our selflessness is but the anticipation of a studded loin of venison. If the truth must be known, when we deign to feed the wild game with hay, mashed potatoes or orange peels, we are engaging less in acts of charity than salving our consciences for pleasures yet to come. The forester wants to care for the game and the hunter wants to shoot it. The one is essential to the other, and it will nothing avail if the game not withstand the bitterest days of winters. Most game are out of season by February. The male and female of fallow deer may not be hunted till July 32, doe and fawn till August 31; chamois are out of season by December 16.

Game feeding-station near Ruhpolding

on the borders of the Chiemgau chalk alps

Frozen Land

The season's victory is complete: the deep temperatures have frozen both the land and the inland waters. Life seems to have withdrawn; everything appears as if it were dead. But we know that this is an appearance that deceives, that nature has taken her precautions and that even a harsh winter can be one of these precautions.

"Winter is a proper man: hard to the core and steadfast" – so the line goes in Matthias Claudius' "Song for Singing behind the Stove":

> "When stone and bone fracture from the frost
> And ponds and lakes are made to crackle . . .

This is the exterior of our scene; the safeguard customary among the North Germans belong indoors. They start with tea every day with a shot of rum and continue with a convivial punch; and the best medicine is a good, stiff grog.

Brunsbüttelkoog, the harbour of the Kiel Canal in wintertime   Iced-in fishery harbour of Friedrichskoog at the mouth of the Elbe

The Joys of Winter

"When will you come again, benign winter that hardens the water for us to resume our dance on skates?" wrote young Wolfgang Goethe in mid-summer of 1773, so much did he yearn for the "ever-recurring verve" ice-skating made him feel. From his poem "Harzreise im Winter" we also know that he was in a position to mount a horse in the middle of winter for a fortnight's ride in the mountains. A winter sportsman, one might say? No, he never heard of the word. Winter sports – skiing, the ski-jump, ice-sailing, curling, ice hockey, bob-sledding and the like – only grew to importance in our century. The major change came when extending the shoes by boards (whence the Scandinavian word "ski") for travel across snow was added to the traditional winter pastimes of skating, sleigh-riding and curling. In Germany the slopes of the Feldberg in the Black Forest were probably the first practice grounds, and the country's first skiing club was founded in the Black Forest in 1893. The yen for this novel type of propulsion spread rapidly; in 1905 the "German Skiing Association" was formed and by 1928 it could count 90,000 members. C. J. Luther's book *"School for Skiing"*, published in 1926, was the ultimate surge in popularizing this pastime, still relatively expensive in those days. Today anyone can afford it and every

Ski-lift to the Grosser Arber in the Bavarian Forest

Skiers on the Wallberg, south of the Tegernsee

major city has its local practice slopes. Skiing grew to be an actual
sport of skill with the advent of jumping, all but a necessity in
steep mountainous terrain. From the following ski-jump records one
may gain an idea of how far this sport has come:

| 1879: | 75.5 ft | 1924: | 302 ft | 1950: | 443 | ft |
| 1900: | 116 ft | 1936: | 331 ft | 1973: | 554.5 ft |

If people once had to wait till the snow fell at their doorsteps, today
countless numbers have both the means to travel where they may
be sure to find snow and the time to stay a while. Nowadays every
third citizen of the Federal Republic takes a winter holiday.

Après-ski

Taking a rest at the Herzogstand Cabin, with a view towards the Benedictine Wall

Olympic Ice Stadium at Garmisch-Partenkirchen

Christmas Letter from a Poet

Heiligenstadt, December 20, 1856

Christmas is coming! My entire house smells of brown cakes –
taken after Mother's receipe – and I have been reposing for a
whole week, so to speak, in the glory of the fir tree. Indeed, whenever I look at my thumb-nail, I note it's half covered with gold. For in
the evening now I only work in gold tinsel, gold crêpe paper and
bright candy wrappers; and while I weave netting and gild fir and
spruce cones and the women, my wife and Rosie, deck out Lisbeth's
doll, Uncle Otto reads to us from Tieck's *Klausenburg* or ever now
and then lets us have a sample from the picture books that will be
put before Hans' and Ernst's plates. Last night I even helped slice up
almonds and candied lemon peels for the Christmas cookies and
threw in a bit of cardamom and sal volatile. In the morning I climbed
around the mountains in the wood to look for fir cones.

Every morning, the last days now, the postman comes and brings
a parcel or a letter from back home or from friends far away. Christmas time is just as marvelous now as it was in my childhood.

(Theodor Storm to his parents)

≪Crèche in the Baroque church at Garmisch

Christmas in Rothenburg-ob-der-Tauber≫

Christmas tree on an island float in Hamburg's Inner Alster

Christmas is Coming

Christmas is seen through radiant eyes; with children this is completely obvious and as for adults, it is because they too were once children. The feelings of the present invoke those of the past and both are met in the gaze of quietly burning candles. The decorated tree binds families together – at least once a year. But since this happens over and over again and often for decades on end, firm traditions find their way into every family and no one dare tamper with them. They begin with the baking recipes for cookies and cakes, proceed to fish or fowl for the "long Christmas meal" and end up with a favourite punch. In between, the actual programme follows its course: listening to the Christmas sermon or attending Midnight Mass, perhaps a Bible lesson read at home (or even avoiding any religious connotation); but in any event there is always "Silent Night", and exchanging gifts and open tokens of mutual love and gratitude. Christmas fulfils the very practical function of reconfirming a sense of home, of knowing where one belongs. Thus this festival is less sentimental than those accoutrements and trappings would lead us to believe that are served up to engender sentimentality. And even the superabundance of gifts and goods – and presents are exchanged in every family and circle of friends – have not been able to eclipse the truer idea of Christmas. Not to those radiant eyes . . .

≪Christ Child Market at Nuremberg

Hamburg's Mönckebergstrasse with Advent decorations

New Year's Eve in Garmisch-Partenkirchen

At the beginning of Advent the concealed and open preparations for the feast of Christmas begin – they being feasts unto themselves. There are minor ones, but no one would want to pass them up; among them are St. Nicholas' Day on December 6 when the good children are rewarded and the bad punished; a first visit to the Christ Child market and ending up by picking out a nice tree; and, of course, the shopping sprees. In honour of the latter, the last three Sundays in Advent used to be termed copper, silver and golden in succession – presumably a reference to how good the turnover was; today, however, shops and stores are open only on the Saturdays in Germany. But this suggestion of cold-nosed commercialism is obviated by the richness of the decorations. And just as Christmas has its forerunners, it also has celebrations to follow, these lasting to the mysteries of Epiphany or Twelfthnight, known in Germany as Three Kings' Day – January 6. Whatever a person dreams on each of the successive twelve nights of Christmas is supposed to come true in each of the twelve months to come, respectively; not only can the weather be prophesized – "How the weather stays till Three Kings' Day, thus it will remain the year away," goes the saying – but also a person's own future; one need only be superstitious enough. In ancient times all weapons and disputes were put aside, for the gods were making their progresses.

Above: Epiphany "Feast of Light" at Pottenstein, Northern Franconia

Winter burnt in effigy at Weinheim-on-the-Bergstrasse≫

Carne Vale

Carnival goes back to a Latin term literally meaning "farewell to meat", because it signals the start of the long Lenten fast, even in a secular form, and because the church kalender calls for this time of abstinence – previously the sacrament of marriage could not be celebrated until Easter, at least no festive weddings. Self-denial is called for, seven long weeks of it. Thus the closer Ash Wednesday is at hand, the more the pleasures of life should be enjoyed with increasing intensity – till the day recalling the transitory nature of life arrives.

In addition to these religiously induced impulses for throwing off inhibitions, still strong despite heavy secularization, there are other ones just as old if not older, natural to man, that fulfil his inclination to a heightened self-consciousness, to forget himself in ecstasy, to climb out of himself, and to free himself of the monotony of the grey-cast day. The most wondrous of these raptures will be presented to him as the gift of fate – that of great love. The others he can contrive for himself, and in this respect his ingenuity will know no bounds. Between the Biblical wine glow of the patriarch Noah and the joints smoked by his progeny seven thousand years later there remains that broad span of yearning to simulate paradises lost with artificial paradises. Thus in the rhythm of the year of every people and nation times of heightened joy are pleasure and allowed for, in which sensible laws permit otherwise sensible citizens to engage in nonsense. To be foolish for three days for the good of one's mental, even political health, to enjoy respite from everyday cares, to put on a costume to give oneself the illusion of being better looking, or younger, or more powerful, to taste of the bliss of anonymous joys while dancing, to let off steam by railing against politics and politicians – these are among the reaons for the artificial paradise of the German Carnival season.

Above: Witches' dance in Upper Swabia

Alemannic Shrovetide Masks≫

The paradise of Carnival is especially cherished in the South-West and along the Rhine, because it is in these regions that the great heritage of the wisdom of Roman government early on found common ground with the heritage of the Church. That that unwritten pact was concluded in token of the vine may be regarded as certain, just as it is certain that the vine is token of Carnival. Wine encourages socialibility, much as Carnival encourages society. Carnival cannot even be imagined under a dictatorship, for the reason that the arrogators of power in such countries aver that an earthly paradise has come into full flourish in their domains in any event, so what else could the people want? As free citizens, we are only too aware of the shortcomings of even the best social order. We talk about it and in Germany, moreover, at Carnival time we ridicule it. "Is a Shrovetide play tantamount to treason? Should we think ill of these cheerful, little rags and tags that might drape the wretched nakedness of our lives in youthful spirits in an enlivening

"Rose Monday" Parade in Cologne, the Monday before Lent

fantasia? If you take life all too seriously, what do you have of it?" Goethe lets his heroic character of Egmont say – and his answer is our answer. We rejoice in these cheerful little rags and tags for but a while, for the duration of the days of clowning – in the classical costume of the clown or in the traditional, popular trappings of the buffoon we enter the pleasure garden of Carnival, where kisses beckon and beckers lure.

Anyone who has ever lost himself in the bustle of Carnival, only he will know to appreciate that self-deprecating wistfulness of that litany struck up before Ash Wednesday looms: "Shrove Tuesday, stay with us . . . Shrove Tuesday, stay with us . . ."

But it avails nothing. Carnival goes by. And then, with the ascent of the year, intimations of other joyful hiatuses in the humdrum of life set in – which is redolent of how Egmont continues his question: "If morning not awaken us to joys new nor evening leave us no desire to hope, then what use of it to get dressed and undressed?"

≪Fasching, the South German term for Carnival, in Munich

"Rose Monday" in Düsseldorf

The Bequest of the Past

Roman Heritage

"One fine day" – it was in the year 58 B. C. – thus Julius Caesar remarked, who held the power over all lands left of the Rhine as part of Roman territory. Was it a fine period? Well, German civilization has had little reason to lament it. Apart from the fact that the Romans with their refined way of life also brought a refined cuisine and introduced the cultivation of wine in the Palatinate, on the Rhine and on the Moselle, they impressed all monuments of ancient civilization on the land. But the fact remains that the Romans stayed with the Germans a good five hundred years, and the fruit of their civilization – some of which were literally in the form of fruit – could ripen to maturity. The Romans built the oldest settlements, such as Baden Baden, and the oldest of German cities, such as Speyer, Worms, Trier and Cologne. In Cologne itself no less than 80,000 artifacts of their daily life have been found and collected. In Trier an entire city gate is still intact; in the village of Igel near Trier there is a commemorative column erected for the venerable house of a family grown rich in the textile trade, and it serves as their grave memorial as well. One old chronicle terms it the "most beautiful pagan monument this side of the Alps" – not to mention the remnants of their temples, villas, baths and aqueducts.

p. 118: The Igel column near Trier; this 72-foot high monument to a Gallo-Roman family dates from the third century A.D.

The Dionysius mosaic at Cologne; part of a Roman villa from the second century A.D., it was discovered during the Second World War in excavating an air-raid shelter in front of the cathedral.

The Porta Nigra in Trier; a castle-gate as part of the Roman town fortifications, it was most probably constructed in the third century A.D.

The following text is carved on the grave marker:

Q POMPEI
VS Q ANIEN
SIS FORO IVLI
BVRRVS M LEX
LEG XV ANN L
STIP XX H S E H F C

T IVLIO TVTTIO T · F
CLAVDIA VIRVNO
MIL LEG XXII PRIMIG
ANN XXXXIII STI

The Youth of Xanten

So different from the Young Siegfried, who steps into the German epic of the *Nibelungenlied* from the Lower Rhenish town of Xanten, a statue of a Young Roman was excavated at a site near Xanten, close on the Dutch border. This is a very real heirloom, not merely a hero of fable. His proportions are also true to life, so humanly orderly and orderly human that any youth of today also stripped of his clothes would in no wise be distinguishable from him. Lost in their thoughts in reflecting about it, we see a group of young girls contemplating in their enlightened manner of today about the perfec-

tion of a culture such as the Romans achieved in the remote colony, so far from their homeland – and so far north of their boundary wall, the "Limes" – and how they could adorn their daily lives with such works of art. For this is no sacred figure or that of a demigod, but merely, as is presumed, a decorative item for a dining-room side-board. At the time this statue was discovered, Xanten was part of Prussia and as a result the original is now located in East Berlin. The *Landesmuseum* in Bonn possesses a bronze cast of it, and another is in the Roman-Germanic Central Museum in Mainz.

Above: Roman grave marker from the Roman-Germanic Museum in Cologne

p. 119: Ruins of the Imperial Roman thermal baths, a gigantic structure dating from the third century A. D.

The "Youth of Xanten"≫

Spirit of the Middle Ages

Clovis, King of the Franks and Lord of Burgundy, Alemannia and Thuringia, accepted Christianity in 496, if for political reasons. It had already risen to be the official religion of Rome. Missionaries came into the country, but they had a difficult time of teaching the Germans to relish a view of the world so foreign to their secular, warlike temperaments. The process of Christianizing them thus took four or five centuries to complete. The coronation of Charlemagne during the Christmas Mass in Rome in the year 800 proclaimed him successor to the Roman Caesars and hastened this process but not ending it. The West – present-day Europe – became Christian. The Middle Ages – "If it were a night, then it was bright as the stars"–manifested itself in all expressions of culture and civilization. Society was separated into its estates, analogous to those of the ecclesiastical hierarchy. Buildings, and most especially churches, gradually grew in splendour with ever increasing ecstasy and fervour of faith into the proportions of cathedrals reaching for the heavens. Wherever one may cast his glance in Germany, one will find an overabundance of structural monuments – both churchly and profane – to those centuries. The museums are filled with the images and altars once removed from the churches and abbeys in an age that had become inimical to imagery. Today even those who no longer have access by faith to this art will treasure them as venerable witnesses to the past and will seek to understand the spirit emanating from them.

Above: Lorsch: Carolingian gate house constructed ca. 800 A.D., one of the best-preserved structures from this period

Regensburg: Imperial Hall in the present-day town hall; here the "Everlasting Imperial Diet", the first German parliament, met from 1663 to 1806.

The Knights and Their Castles

Knights belong with castles. The military system of the Middle Ag was also a feudal system; anyone enfeoffed with property was obliged to bear his appropriate share of military service and expenses in return. In those times military service meant cavalry service. The knights, invested with most of the surrounding land, represented the professional soldiers of their day. When they were summoned to join with their French counterparts in the Crusades t conquer the Holy Land and to ward off the spread of Islam, their profession rose higher in esteem. Even if the goals of the Crusade: were not fully attained, the encounters of the German knights with

≪Hornberg Castle on the Neckar. Seat of the Imperial Knight and leader in the Peasants' War, Götz von Berlichingen, he died here in 1562.

Eltz Castle on the Moselle (13th – 16th centuries), one of the most picturesque cas settings in Germany≫

Below: Baronial hall of the lake-moated castle of Linn near Krefeld

the French made them more susceptible to the beauties and graces of life; we need only think of the *Minnesänger,* the courtly poets of the High Middle Ages, to gain an idea of how the Crusades broadened their horizons. Knightly castles became repositories of culture and civilization. The visage of the "Bamberg Knight" epitomizes the ideal of knighthood in the Hohenstaufen period. The decline of knighthood is tokened by the "robber barons", who with their armed hordes attacked travelling merchants. The Thirty Years' War cast most of the feudal castles into ruins.

Werenwag Castle on the Upper Danube; dating from the 11th century, it is now in the possession of the princes of Fürstenberg.

≪Inner court of Coburg Castle, the main portions of which, however, did not arise until the 16th century. The apartments of the present ducal family are located in the "Princes' Wing"; precious collections of art and ancient relics are on display in the other quarters.

The Castle of Nuremberg, a wide-ranging structure dating from the 11th to the 13th centuries and consisting of three groups of buildings: the Imperial Stables, the Burgrave Castle and the Imperial Castle. In the possession of the burgraves of Nuremberg, a branch of the Swabian House of Hohenzollern since 1192, it was sold to the City in 1427.≫

Early Churches

The architecture of the first major Christian edifices on German soil is modelled on that of the Roman basilica. The first public worship services of the early Christians were held in basilicas, often the porticos of the great Roman patrician houses. At the time the basilica was adopted by the German master builders, it was developed into an elongated building having a central nave higher than the aisles. It is characterized by the rounded arch. This elongated structure got to be divided into nave and two or even four aisles by columns supporting such rounded arches. Toward the end of the eleventh century the flat wooden roofs common until then were replaced with vaulted roofs of stone, the first major alteration to grow to be the traditional pattern. It was not until 1825 that general agreement led to terming this style dating from Merovingian times "Romanesque"; later the Gothic style with its pointed arches succeeded it. It is

Above: St. George's, Oberzell, on the Isle of Reichenau on Lake Constance, late Carolingian, dating from 900

≪Collegiate Church at Freckenhorst, known as the "Westphalian Peasants' Cathedral", most portion of which date from the 11th and 12th centuries

The Collegiate Church at Corvey-on-the-Weser; the west front, from 873, is the oldest preserved edifice in Westphalia.≫

possible to study the Romanesque on German soil in all its phases. Among the very early examples are St. Michael's Chapel in Fulda, with its crypt dating from 820–822, the Collegiate Church in Gernrode, begun in 961, St. Michael's, Hildesheim, from 1033, and the cathedral at Paderborn, from 1068. The cathedrals on the Rhine at Speyer, Worms and Mainz are majestic examples of Romanesque at its height. But as is so often the case, here we may also sense the charm of first flower, a keen devotion at the beginning that is stronger than when seen in the perfection of maturity. To which day did the star-bright night of the Middle Ages yield? We call it the modern age and the hesitation with which we refer to it is evidence of the fact that we are unable to forget the harmony of art and life in the past above the stormy progress of our epoch. We do know,

however, how high a price man has had to pay for this process of reaching his maturity. It has lasted many centuries and still has not reached completion. Nevertheless, dating the ages is flexible; no page of the calendar tells the end of the Middle Ages or the beginning of the modern era. Opinion even varies as to whether the date for the beginning of the Middle Ages should be set with the onset of the great migrations or the end of the Roman Empire in the West, or whether the arrival of modern times can be dated from the discovery of America or with the appearance of Luther. The consciousness of life is in constant flux; since it is most clearly expressed in the architecture of a given day, one will do well to inquire after the spirit that governed life in generations past and that gave rise to their buildings.

Königslutter, cloister of the Romanesque Collegiate Church, as completed by Henry the Lion in the last quarter of the 12th century

≪St. Michael's, Hildesheim, a former Benedictine abbey church, one of the most magnificent of Romanesque basilicas in Germany; it was begun in the 11th century, renovated in the 12th century and subsequently altered on a number of occasions.

Baroque Splendour

Churches are built by the spirit of piety, but this spirit is constantly in a process of change. Martin Luther's Reformation had a deep, incisive effect in that piety was shifted to the inner being of each individual man, and no external attributes, vestments, paintings or images were necessary any longer. Churches should become barren and sober. But the Reformation gave cause to the Counter-Reformation, and to put this view to spite: everywhere it asserted itself churches, abbeys and convents – to cite the phrase of the poetess Ricarda Huch – set out to "don the regalia of the victor." To this urge we owe a number of churches that are the embodiment of splendour. In addition, there came a further impulse. After the devastation and plunder of the Thirty Years' War it was necessary to think of reconstruction. The dark years had passed and a new and joyous sense of life spread through the land, together with a sense of gratitude for sheer survival. In terms of architecture we call its exponent "Baroque" and the later, even more festive and jubilant manifestation of this style, "Rococo". It is no coincidence that it is three churches favoured for pilgrimages that represent among the most notable examples of the latter style: the church of the Cistercian convent at Birnau on Lake Constance; the Pilgrim Church of the "Fourteen Helpers in Distress" in Upper Franconia, subsequently of the "Fourteen Saints"; and the Pilgrim Church of St. Mary's-in-the-Meadow of the Hostaged Saviour in the famous "Priest's Corner", which, like the Rococo church at Rottenbuch and the Romanesque abbey church at Steingaden with its interior transformed into Rococo, is a magnificent specimen of this style. It was intended that the pilgrims should return home with an indelible picture of grandeur and the new beauty of their faith.

The Pilgrim Church of St. Mary's-in-the-Meadow, constructed between 1746 to 1754 and the masterpiece of Dominikus Zimmermann. It is one of the most mature achievements of the Bavarian Rococo. The stucco work and ceiling frescoes are the work of Johann Baptist Zimmermann, the architect's brother.

The collegiate church at Rottenbuch-on-the-Ammer, a late Romanesque structure transformed into the Baroque style between 1737 and 1742 by J. Schmuzer ▷

Proud Townsmen

The burgher spirit created the towns and cities of Germany, caused them to grow and flourish. The sense of community keep rein on the mercantile instincts. The town was protected by wall and moat, and guarded by tower and gate. A community had to seek its own protection for life and death in case of siege. But this was the exception, not the rule. The expression "town air is liberating" refers to the privileges accorded to the inhabitants of the town – to hold markets and fairs, to be granted their own constitutions and courts. Even such freedoms as these found their own expression in architecture. And this was always most convincing in the town halls whenever they may have been built; the oldest are in Lübeck, Münster and Ulm. But no matter what the style, the town halls always stand for civic pride and self-assertion. During the restoration of Mainz's town hall destroyed in wartime a plaque was laid which proclaimed: "Here the City of Mainz is building a town hall for its citizens, the first since 1462: Symbol of the City's vitality in its third millennium". May not one apply that sense that pride thus spoken to all towns and cities? The pride in being a born and bred citizen of Munich, of Frankfurt, of Cologne or of Hamburg has not waned any less than it has in any other town citizens.

Burghausen-on-the-Salzach, with its extensive castle grounds. This town of Upper Bavaria with its ancient houses is typical of Italian architectural influence in towns along the Rivers Inn and Salzach.

≪Regensburg, with its Stone Bridge, dating from the 12th century, and its Cathedral, built between the 13th and 16th centuries

Augsburg: the town hall, a Renaissance building erected by the municipal architect Elias Holl from 1615 to 1620; foreground: the Franciscan Convent Church of Maria Stella.

Velberg in the Bühlertal, with its castle, town walls, gates and bulwarks

Altensteig, an ancient town in the Upper Nagold Valley of the Black Forest

Imperial Merchants

The House of Fugger, one of the most inestimably rich of merchant families, and located in Augsburg, did not merely *fugger,* as the slang term in German indicates to mean conducting business with extremely sharp acumen, but they also invested large amounts of their profits in fixtures which were intended for the common good. As did numerous other patrician families in Augsburg, they built palaces and donated church buildings. The chapel at St. Anna's in Augsburg, which Jakob, known as "the Rich" (1459–1525), had built, is the first Renaissance building on German soil. They founded great libraries and art collections. In short, like the great American, entrepreneurs of a later age and in Germany the Krupp, Thyssen and Volkswagen Foundations have done, they took upon themselves the worthy office of promoting culture. As to their obligations to their fellowmen, they could feel they were upholding them – as have done their successors – in a form utterly novel for their time. Jakob Fugger went one step further in building a separate housing estate for the poorer citizens. It consists of 106 apartments, spread over 53 small houses. These represent the first row houses any-where as well as the first of all welfare housing to be built. Jakob had them built between 1516 and 1525, at the time he was "financing" the election of Charles V as Holy Roman Emperor – not exactly a self-serving deed if one considers that Francis I of France

Above: Augsburg, Hall of Mirrors in the Palais Schaezler, the most splendid of the city's patrician houses; built between 1765 and 1767 by Karl A. von Lespilliez of the court of the Elector in Munich for the banker von Liebert

Schöntal Abbey on the River Jagst: staircase of the new abbey, the work of J. L. Dientzenhofer; ca. 1750≫

Rothenburg-ob-der-Tauber, the most famous and picturesque of the ancient Imperial cities; it has remained all but completely intact since the Thirty Years' War.

An old lane in Bad Wimpfen on the River Neckar; background: the Blue Tower, once part of the town fortifications≫

was the rival candidate. As banker to the Pope this one Fugger also had his hand in the notorious sales of indulgences in 1517. But such activities, including the welfare estate known as the *Fuggerei,* were mere sidelines for him. The Fuggers made most of their money by holding the European monopoly on copper. They gained control of the richest deposits all the way from Hungary to Spain and this done, they were able to dictate the price. In addition, they had been engaged in the spice trade from the East Indies as early as 1505; in this field they found competition from another Augsburg merchant family, the Welsers. They owe their property holdings, extensive even today, to the "Imperial shortage of cash" – they took land as security for each loan they made to the Emperor. The Term "royal merchant" had not been coined at the time, but by analogy one could certainly call Jakob Fugger an Imperial merchant. There is a portrait of him by Dürer.

Deidesheim-on-the-Weinstrasse, with the 16th century town hall and the Gothic parish church

Mainz Cathedral, which together with those at Worms and Speyer represents the apex of Romanesque architecture in the central and upper districts of the Rhine; it was built in the 11th–13th centuries.

Princely Seats
Spiritual and Temporal

The cathedral, often called minster in South Germany, is the church of a bishop; it contains his episcopal throne, the *cathedra,* or seat, whether bishop or archbishop. Since the bishops are considered to be the direct successors of the Apostles, their churches reflect outside and in the high dignity of their office. In Germany there was the additional factor that the holders of the episcopals sees of Mainz, Trier and Cologne also occupied the high temporal ranks of Elector Princes with the right of participating in the election of the Holy Roman Emperor. Along with them a number of bishops and archbishops were "immediate", i. e. sovereign unto themselves, owing only direct allegiance to the Emperor. Accordingly, most cathedrals will have their counterparts in the temporal gubernatorial seats of the bishops, their palaces. Bruchsal Palace belonged to Speyer Cathedral, Palais Favorite to Mainz, and that at Brühl to Cologne; in Würzburg the palace is located within the confines of the city. Cathedrals and minsters were built "to the glory of God" – projects in which entire generations on end took part. Freiburg Minster is the one built entirely in the age of Gothic. The bishops built their residential palaces to their own glory; since they were elected to the rank of prince, their title could not be bequeathed and they had to provide for their own monuments during their lifetimes. For them their palaces were their most precious commemorations to their name.

Next in rank to the bishops were the abbots in charge of the abbeys. Originally the title applied only to abbeys of the Benedictines, but was later applied to other orders as well. Even some abbots enjoyed the privileges of "Imperial immediacy", i. e., they were also temporal princes. Their revenues befitted such rank, and among the richest of abbeys were those of the Cistercians at Ebrach in Franconia and of the Benedictines at Corvey, near Höxter-on-the-Weser. But even the smaller sovereign abbeys owned lands in abundance, these ever being added to by gifts and bequeathals, and with the revenues from them and the fruits of their own efforts abbey churches of extraordinary splendour could be built. Such magnificance, gaining momentum in the Baroque period and reaching its peak in the Rococo, was not self-seeking; it was so "that God be glorified above all", as the rule of the Benedictine Order phrases it; it served in the Counter-Reformation as a propaganda device as well. The best architects, builders, painters and master craftsmen were adequate to the task of fashioning earthly intimations of the bliss of heaven on high.

Church of the Fourteen Saints, a pilgrimage site near Lichtenfels-on-the-Main; built 1743–1772 by Balthasar Neumann

Ochsenfurt, the "new" town hall (1497–1513) on the market place with its ornate outdoor staircase

Panorama of Bamberg, the ancient Franconian Imperial city and episcopal see, with its cathedral, palace, the Michaelsberg and Old Town Hall (pp. 148–149)

Route of German History: the River Main

Is it not right and proper in promoting tourism to combine the sequences of scenic beauties, historical monuments, not to speak of the tempting delights of the palate all together into "routes"? This mode of presentation so useful to the traveller is especially apt for southern Germany, where he can rove along the Weinstrasse, the Nibelungenstrasse, or the Romantic Road or the Swabian Baroque Route. The epitome of such routes is the Bergstrasse, a gift of nature, between Darmstadt and Heidelberg. But often the courses of rivers may also represent a manner of natural route, along which the attractions of beauty, art and history may be gathered. The most renowned example of this are the reaches of the Rhine between Bingen and Koblenz. If we speak of the "Weser Renaissance", we mean the architectural monuments clustered along this river. The River Main also is a route in that particular sense of there being no other term quite so fitting and illustrative of the fact that this river, in the heart of the country, reflects German domestic history like no other; the Rhine is more indicative of Germany's international role. The Main's alluring shores are plainly inducive to making settlements and these banks have witnessed the domination of monks, knights and burghers, of Imperial coronations and peasants' revolts. From its source, or the confluence of its two sources, to its mouth, the river in its entirety is reader and textbook unto itself of German

history – certainly down to 1848. Along with that delegation commissioned by the Diet of the German Federation meeting in Frankfurt's St. Paul's Church to travel to Berlin to offer the German Imperial crown to the King of Prussia went Germany's fate from the Main to the River Spree as well. What remains is the Main itself, the route along which from Bamberg to Frankfurt's Old City hamlet and town and city are aligned like pearls on a string, and all are marked by both the glories and burdens of German history.

Above: The Bamberg Knight, by an unknown master of ca 1240; the Adam Portal and Prince's Gate are also by his hand.

≪ Ebrach in the Steigerwald: rose window of the early Gothic church of the Cistercian Abbey

Centerpiece of the Veit Stoss altar in Bamberg Cathedral≫

Old Half-Timbered Towns

The charm of old German towns, as seen on the Main and north and south of it, lies in their half-timbered houses. Half-timber construction may be termed the peasants' type of architecture; it was adopted by townsmen, because it was a cheap way of building. Churches, castles, palaces and town halls were built of stone, which often had to be transported to the construction site at a much higher cost. Schiller was born in a village half-timbered cottage, Goethe in a stone town house. But because the material was cheap, it did not preclude turns of the imagination. Half-timbered houses appear in innumerable variations, from the simple that tell only of their function to the over-ornate, even prodigiously lavish that are expressions both of function, as with a town hall or guild house, and of pride. And they will reveal their origin in time through the style in which they were built. They exist in every sort of style; there are Gothic as well as Baroque half-timbered structures. One disadvantage of them is their susceptibility to fire. A house of stone will be gutted, but a half-timber will burn to the ground. For this reason entire quarters of town could be kindled by fire; thus the figure of the night watchman was a fixture of every town of half-timbered houses. He made his rounds less as a protector of public morals than as someone keeping an eye of the chimneys and the first sign of spreading flame.

Fritzlar: market place with fountain and half-timbered houses

Michelstadt in the Odenwald: the town-hall; begun in 1484 it is the oldest oaken building in Germany

The Austere Charm of North Germany

All half-timbered structures are gabled buildings, houses with roofs. This basic pattern is repeated individually in both street and square. Individuality means not arbitrariness, but implies adaptation to the individual street or individual square. A house facing the market place will have different proportions and a different façade from a house on the edge of town. The uniformity of the basic pattern, taken together with an implicitly understood adaptation to the fabric of the town as an entity, even of the village, creates that manner of harmony we appreciate all the more the less able we are to reconjure it in our present ways of building. The half-timbered cores of South German towns still in a state of good preservation, especially their opulent market places, seem not only more ornate than their North German counterparts, but also more zestful. But the northern variety emanates a charm of its own, if more subdued. It bespeaks a restrained gracefulness that prefers to conceal its opulence rather than put it on display. One first thinks of these towns when the German eighteenth century comes to mind; they are the poet Gleim's Halberstadt, the critic Lessing's Wolfenbüttel, the philosopher Lichtenberg's Göttingen, and the Bückeburg of Goethe's polymath mentor Herder. These are the towns hat have formed the true dwelling place of the German civic spirit.

Above: Lüneburg staircase to the Princes' Hall in the town hall

Paderborn: Abdinghof Church (11th century) and cathedral (11th to 13th centuries)

The Roland statue in front of the Bremen town hall, symbol of the high jurisdiction entailed in the city's independence (p. 156)

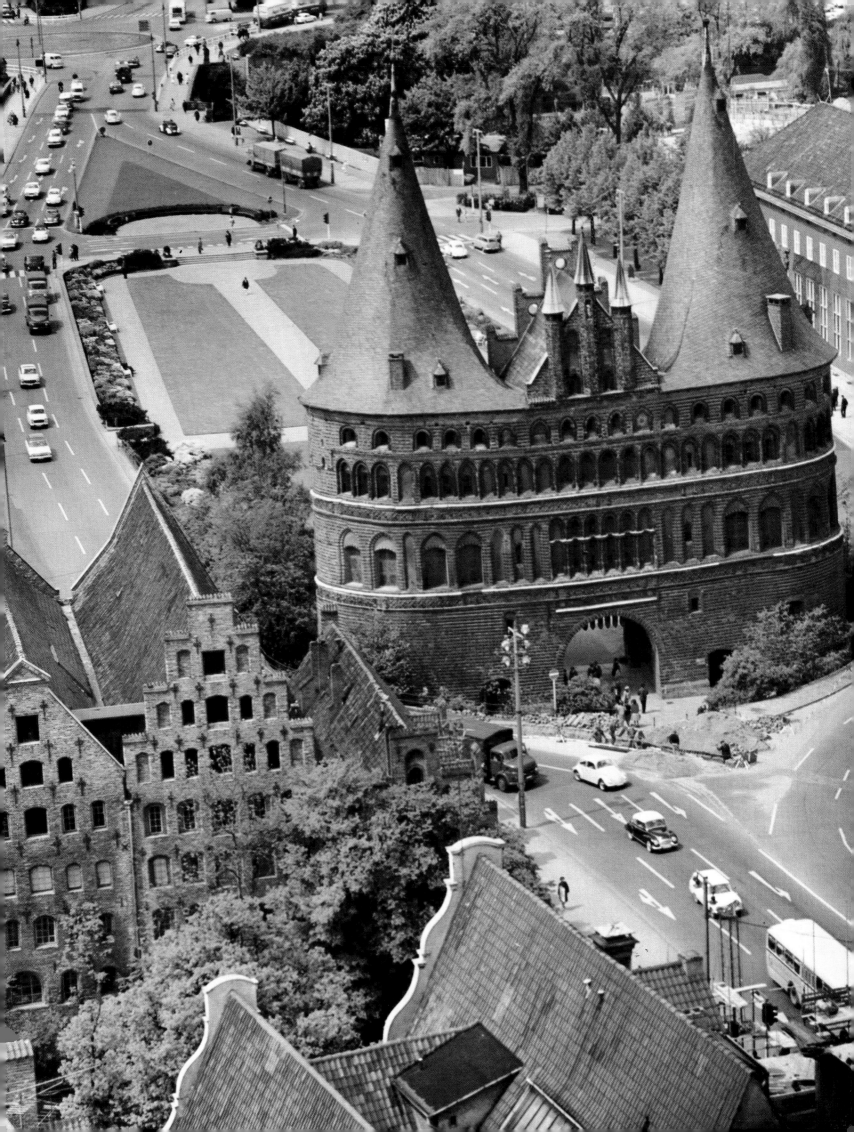

Emden: town hall and harbour gate on the Delft (1635)

The Holsten Gate at Lübeck, completed in 1477; it is the grandest of all town gates in Germany (p. 157)

Xanten: old mill on the town walls and the Klever Gate (1393)

Neresheim's Example

The restoration of the Benedictine abbey church at Neresheim, near Nördlingen, founded in 1095 and enjoying Imperial sovereignty, was entrusted to Balthasar Neumann, the most renowned architect of his day. The commission was given in 1747; after the designs had been prepared, the cornerstone was laid in 1750. But three years later the architect died. Although the construction had to be completed by other masters and despite the fact that its adornment had to be made simpler, a church arose here, about which the art historian Dehio could say: "Baroque architecture not only in Germany, but in all Europe, has little that can measure up to this structure." After being secularized Neresheim came into the possession of the princes of Thurn and Taxis, who shortly afterwards, in 1807, declared: "The beautiful church is there; to let it fall into disrepair would be regarded by the present world and the world to come as sheer barbarism." Starting with a thorough renovation of the frame of the roof that had to support no less than seven cupolas, the princes sought to ward off such "barbarism" by the year 1828 Meanwhile, because the cupola vaulting had been done in wood and not in stone as Balthasar Neumann had wanted it, increasingly more pronounced cracks were appearing in the frescoes over the course of a century and a half through the natural aging of the wood. In 1903 a fine wire net was stretched across the plaster of the great paintings beneath the cupolas "to prevent the fresco surfaces from collapsing under pressure." This ad hoc solution could not last forever. The cracks grew larger. The suction and pressure from supersonic flights exacerbated the danger of collapse. On June 13, 1966 the church was closed on police orders. Ever since then the edifice has been under renovation literally from the ground up as probably no church fabric has ever experienced. Neresheim is being rescued; the structure is being reinforced principally by inserting steel anchors into the masonry and placing a new frame of steel over the main cupola; the frescoes of the cupolas are being safeguarded by strengthening the lamination and removing the lead white in the paint. Neresheim is being spared, even if at a cost of some DM 15 million.

Benedictine abbey at Neresheim and church

Restorer at work on one of the church ceilings

Neresheim, the abbey church scaffolded within and without (pp. 161–162)

Princely Palaces

Palace – today one might never want to pass one up, whether spiritual or temporal, whether in the midst of a city or in a park. Yet we know that they merely represent the glittering showy aspect of the actual curse of past history in Germany – of the plethora of small states that once made up the Empire. After the end of the Thirty Years' War, in a time of reconstructing and replanning villages, cities, churches and palaces, a new spirit raged over Europe with the appearance of Louis XIV in France, the spirit of absolutism. A prince would regard himself "by the grace of God" the sole incorporation of the State. He was not timorous about his affinity to God – quite the contrary, he emphasized it in his ceremonial designed to emulate the heavenly hosts. This presumptuous idea found its

Berlin: view from the park of Charlottenburg Palace, built by Nering and Eosander von Göthe between 1695–1712 under Frederick I, continued under Frederick the Great by Georg Wenzeslaus von Knobelsdorff between 1740–1743, and completed in 1788 by Carl Gotthard Langhans.

Lake-moated castle of Lembeck in the Münster area: begun in the 14th century, by 1962 it hadbeen completed in keeping with its original character of the type of castle by the last representative of the von Westerholt family. It has been in the possession of the Merveldt family since 1708. (pp. 164–165).

quintessence in the Palace of Versailles, the central edifice of the centre of authority of the French monarchs. In Germany, where three hundred fifty courts were maintained – disregarding many more a sovereign that could not afford his own court – not only was French taste adopted in all aspects of life, understandable after such a prolonged and barbaric war, not only was French adopted as the language of cultivation, but many a ruler wanted to have his own Versailles since he ruled "by the grace of God" just as did *le roi soleil.* But a mini-Versailles was not good enough for them; they

wanted to go it one better. Even Frederick the Great made fun of this vanity – but not enough to keep him from building his vast palace "Sanssouci" at Potstam. Yet Frederick had power in the back of him; but what power stood, say, behind Duke Charles II August of Palatinate-Zweibrücken? He built his palace, known as "Karlsberg" and destroyed in 1793, with the intention of outdoing Versailles. In any event it at least surpassed the French model in the number of stalls, to keep 1,500 horses, of kennels, to accommodate 1,000 hunting dogs, plus a barracks for 600 men.

Weissenstein-ob-Pommersfelden Palace: the staircases, built between 1711-1718 by Johann Dientzenhofer, at the commission of Lothar Franz, episcopal Prince of Bamberg and concurrently Elector and Archbishop of Mainz, as well as Arch-Chancellor of the Holy Roman Empire.

Archiepiscopal Palace at Würzburg: Imperial Hall; this gigantic Baroque edifice was begun in the early 18th century under the episcopal Prince Johann Philipp Franz Graf von Schönborn following the plans of Balthasar Neumann and was not completed until 1779.

Weikersheim Palace: hunting and baronial hall, built between the 16th and 18th centuries; panelled ceiling by Elias Gunzenhäuser; paintings in the ceiling panels by Balthasar Katzenberger

Stuttgart: the Old Palace, begun in the 16th century by the Dukes Christoph and Ludwig on the old foundations of a moated castle

Munich: Nymphenburg Palace, begun between 1663 and 1728 by Agostino Barelli and comissioned by the Electress Adelaide of Savoy; resumed in 1674 by Enrico Zuccalli and completed in 1675. Under Max Emanuel it was expanded by G. A. Viscardi and Josef Effner (pp. 170–171).

If we recall that the construction of Versailles was begun in 1661, we may well understand that most palaces built in Germany in this mould were not under construction until the 18th century. It was not long before the palace meant more than the symbol of princely omnipotence; if at Versailles the sovereign had a park lay at his feet, in Germany it had to be an entire city. If none were already there, then a city was founded. One example of this is Karlsruhe, started in 1715 by the Margave Karl Wilhelm of Baden-Durlach. The basic fan-shaped outline of the city was meant to serve no other purpose. It will be obvious that the German princes would not have waited for construction on Versailles to begin, for even Versailles had its antecedents in the Baroque palaces of Italy. Thus it happened that it also was Italian architects that built the first Baroque palaces in Germany – right about the time of Versailles, such as Nymphenburg at Munich, dating from 1663, and Herrenhausen at Hannover, from 1665.

Bavaria's Royal Palaces

In 1777 Carl Theodor, Elector of the Palatinate, assumed the Electorate of Bavaria through inheritance. He came from a collateral line of the Wittelsbachs, themselves no less keen on building. Carl Theodor's father had built Mannheim Palace, which with its 1500 windows is the largest such edifice on German soil, as well as the city of the same name. As previously in Mannheim, Carl Theodor reigned in Munich as an absolute sovereign with the rank of prince; and this predilection remained in the blood of his successors when Bavaria became a kingdom on 1806 by grace of Napoleon. Ludwig I commissioned the magnificent buildings that established Munich's representations as a city of the arts. His grandson, Ludwig II, the "Romantic King", felt that he sat so less

"by the grace of God" on the throne of Bavaria. In token of this he had the palace at Herrenchiemsee built, the ultimate copy of Versailles in the German realms, also the weakest imitation, because it is devoid of soul. Prior to this he had built Linderhof, also an imitatio in this instance of a Rococo palace. But it is Neuschwanstein that reveals his true innermost fancies. Constructed on the ruins of the former castle of Schwanstein and in the immediate vicinity of another royal palace, Hohenschwangau, built by his father, it shows Ludwig II's tastes to be neo-Romantic on the exterior and Gothic within. Frescoes from the motifs of Wagner's operas may be seen in the extravagant inner chambers – as an entity it is a fond divination of a German past that never truly existed.

Herrenchiemsee Palace, begun in 1878 by Georg Dollmann at the commission of Bavaria's King Ludwig II, in imitation of Versailles. Construction remained incomplete following the King's death in 1886. (Air-photo courtesy of the government of Upper Bavaria, No. G 43/1125).

Neuschwanstein Castle, near Füssen, built between 1869–1886 under Ludwig II

Cities — Savouring the Old Among the New

Since the reconstruction of German cities destroyed in the Second World War was not something that could be accomplished overnight, there was ample time to give deep thought as to how it should be done. Should the devastated city centres be built in their historical pattern to give new buildings the outer shell of the old façades, as was done in Münster, or should they be chock-full of modern architecture, without any heed to tradition? The latter choice was followed in rebuilding the Römerberg in Frankfurt am Main. But it was also Frankfurt that furnished an example, hotly contested at the time, of a restoration true to the original down to the last detail – that of Goethe's birthplace "Zu den drei Leyern" in a street known as Grosser Hirschgraben. For this undertaking careful planning had long been made. The house, object of many a Goethe admirer's pilgrimage, had been closed during the War. Its entire contents – furniture, paintings, books from the adjacent Goethe Museum, even patterns of the wallpaper were stored in safety and survived the destruction and plunder of the War unscathed. In so doing the effect could be achieved that any visitor today to the Goethe house will gain the impression that he is seeing the original building, its furbishings completely intact. In such a manner the city's new buildings arose, streets and squares – all based on the subterranean infrastructure of the town, its vital arteries of sewerage systems, water and gas conduits, and electric cables. But the bridges and train stations could not be dismantled without waiving resources worth millions that remained in the form of piers and railway tracks. But in this case there was no compelling reason to

Panorama of Frankfurt am Main, showing the Cathedral (right), and St. Paul's Church and the town hall, the *Römer* (left)

175

Munich: Ludwigstrasse, showing the University (at right) and St. Ludwig's Church

follow any particuar architectural form in rebuilding such structures
and the laws of the free market – supply and demand – prevailed.
And the demand for housing and office space grew from year
to year. The end result, by and large attractive, is there for all to
see in the skyline of any German city, where high office blocks and
multi-storeyed dwelling automats predominate. The church towers
that once were the chief landmark of the silhouette of any city or
town now occupy only a modest position, and in many places it will
be the television towers with their rotating restaurants that tell of a
new era. The old is juxtaposed against the new.

Munich Beer

Munich – Germany's "cosmopolis with a heart" as it likes to hear itself called – is the capital of beer, no matter what. Even if more beer may be brewed and drunk in other cities, in Munich beer is glorified, as in the Hofbräuhaus, its temple on earth. This citadel devoted to beer is a state-run institution. Up until the 16th century the people of Munich drank a heavy barley beer, of which the less said the better. When they were introduced to a light beer produced in Bohemia, they succeeded in striking a balance between the old and the new and came up with a compromise, known as brown beer. Now this was "too good a thing simply to benefit the people," so it was only brewed for the court. In order to fill the state coffers,

however, as of 1610 it was sold to the public and traded. The fame of beer from Munich went forth all over the world. Both the state of Bavaria and the city of Munich still cash in on this even today. But, leaving the consistently high quality of the beer aside, times have changed. Munich, the giant village until only the recent past, has grown to be a metropolis of over a million people. The new underground railway is its new landmark; it travels to all the older landmarks – the English Garden, the Victory Gate, the Isar, fresh as a mountain stream, the Deutsches Museum, and to Schwabing, that artists' quarter still preserved in the middle of town – now revealing even greater charms.

Munich: Arabellahaus

Munich: pedestrian zone showing the Neuhauserstrasse and Karl's Gate

Stuttgart Spätzle

The line the River Main draws straight across Germany may also be looked upon as a dividing line of German food habits. North of it the potato reigns supreme as the basic foodstuff and south of it farinaceous foods. As a matter of fact, South German food cannot be conceived of without Bavarian scrambled pancakes and Swabian *Spätzle*. And being the capital of Swabia, Stuttgart has managed to assert itself admirably as the capital city of this dish. It is made of a dough consisting of meal, eggs, water and salt that rolled flat on a board is then shredded into boiling water. *Spätzle* goes well with Sauerbraten, not to say Sauerkraut with pork or lentils and sausage. There is no limit of ways it can be used. A rustic dish that has found its niche in the big city is not an everyday phenomenon. This tells us something of the Stuttgarters and is revelant of the reason why Stuttgart is known as the largest small town in Germany. Life is not hectic in this metropolis, as it well is, of which the symbol is its oft-copied television tower; it is friendly and easy-going. The native Swabian diligence can afford this attitude toward life. Meanwhile, Stuttgart has always done well and always kept pace with things; admittedly it has been constantly enlivened by the Swabian talents for invention and enterprise. It is thus that Stuttgart has become the home base of the Mercedes and Bosch industries, to mention but two of a great many more.

Stuttgart: the Schulstrasse transformed into a pedestrian street and shopping centre

"Half a Chicken" in Cologne

The visitor is confronted with the city's impressive past glories no sooner has he stepped out of the central station. There the mighty cathedral towers up before him; planned and begun in medieval times only to be completed in the 19th century, it lies at the foot of the ever-lively Hohe Strasse, of which it is claimed with pride that it has changed neither in direction or purpose for two thousand years. And in the immediate vicnty the home bases may be found of eau de Cologne and of the *Gürzenich,* the festive dancing hall of this happy-go-lucky city. What do the people like to drink? A *Kölsch,* of course – a most pala-table type of top-fermented beer. It goes well with what they call "half a chicken" – a plain rye bun, or *Röggelchen,* without butter and covered with a sturdy, old Dutch cheese – but definitely not anything resembling one-half a roast chicken.

Above: Cologne's Schildergasse as a pedestrian zone

Cologne: pedestrian zone at the Cathedral

Cologne: Rhine panorama, showing the Cathedral and St. Martin's Church; far right: the main railway station (pp. 180–181)

Düsseldorf Apple Tarts

Heinrich Heine was born in Düsseldorf and grew up there. All his life he was proud of this city – even if in the hope that people there one day would also be proud of him – and the memory of it dwelt in his heart. For what reason? It was the apple tarts that got to him: "There by the corner of the theatre the marvelously wizened fellow with his sabre-like legs stood in a white apron holding a basket around him full of lovely, steaming apple tarts . . . In those days apple tarts were my passion – now it consists of love, truth, freedom and crayfish soup . . ."

Were Heine to return today, he would not recognize modern Düsseldorf. He would marvel at the elegance of the Königsallee, visit the new theatre, look around the museums and art galleries – in Düsseldorf the greatest collection of Gotheana is gathered in the Kippenberg Collection – but once in the Old Town his heart would well up again. It has been restored. But it did not turn into a dead relic of the past, but is a quarter of town made bustling and full of life by the young people who frequent it, indeed bursting with happiness and pleasure.

Düsseldorf: outdoor restaurant in the Königsallee

Düsseldorf: the Thyssen Block (302 feet high; 25 storeys)

Hamburg Eel Soup

In the *ABC of Cookery*, the cookery book of grandmother's day, published by Carl Habel of Berlin in 1902, the recipe for a proper Hamburg eel soup was revealed – plus what it would cost to serve four people. This pleasure, including two pears stewed in white wine and sugar or twelve prunes – would amount to two marks thirty-two pfennigs. It does not come this cheap any more, but the citizenry of Hamburg still like to have it. Their yen for eel soup is one of the more amiable notes of the Hamburg tradition.

Hamburg is a city-state unto itself; and as many faces as this city may present to the visitor, they all hark back to the traditions of its history. It is the proud history of the mercantile spirit, of derring-do far across the seas. It is the Hanseatic spirit that is not easily suppressed and that insists on its own independence even today. St. Pauli, the entertainment quarter, belongs to the international port of Hamburg, not to the smart circles that hold season tickets to the State Opera, the Schauspielhaus or the Thalia-Theater. And German television viewers are all patrons of the Ohnsorg-Theater that glorifies everyday life in Hamburg in its pleasant suburban episodes, much as eel soup serves to do by other means.

Hamburg's harbour with a view of the inner city and the River Alster (air-photo courtesy government of Upper Bavaria, No. G 43/630; pp. 186–187)

≪Hamburg: Nikolaifleet, one of the Hanseatic city's few remaining house-lined canals

Hamburg: the Ost-West-Strasse, with a view of St. Michael's Church and the tower of St. Nikolai's, destroyed in the Second World War≫

Berlin: Kurfürstendamm, showing the Café Kranzler and the Kaiser Wilhelm Memorial Church

Berlin White Beer

At the beginning of the nice time of year when people can sit out of doors, Berlin's own beverage *Weisse,* or white beer, comes into its own. A top-fermented brew, it is low in alcoholic content and fizzy, hence refreshing. It is drunk in a large thick goblet and a "shot" of raspberry syrup or woodruff is added. The sweet and sour combination is just right. But is that not indicative of Berlin's character? Of its innate steadfastness combined with a shot of true wit? As the seat of the Electors of Brandenburg, later the kings of Prussia, this city, ever upright and sober, "fasted itself to greatness" along with the Prussian State and for three quarters of a century assumed the role of capital of the German Reich – with an Imperial Palace and Imperial Diet and with an economic burgeoning beyond compare. The political dégringolade of 1918 was followed by a cultural and artistic efflorescence that was the product of the new freedoms. Berlin became Germany's premier theatrical city, film-making centre, literary Mecca, and musical capital. The "Golden Twenties" had emerged. But today, along with a visible wall, an intangible wall traverses the city. Yet despite this, or because of this, the new Berlin with its imposing vitality, is ever worth a visit. The Kurfürstendamm has become the most fascinating of German streets – not least because it is the most cosmopolitan.

Berlin: central plaza of the Europa Centre

Berlin:
the AVUS motorway
and *Funkturm*

The Vital Present

Satellites of the City Centre

The term "satellite" coming from Latin originally meant a follower or retainer, i.e., a subordinate dependent upon a man of higher rank. We may consider many countries of Eastern Europe to be satellites of the Soviet Union. In outer space the moon is still regarded as the most consequential satellite of the earth – the only natural one among the many artificial satellites. To the categories of subordinate men and nations we may add the subordinate municipalities that are satellites of the older cities. This is not a very felicitous choice of term, nor is it fully accurate. What previously was known as the sub-urbs or later dormitory towns has been upgraded in name and height although satellite towns are still nothing more than residential developments in easy reach of the inner city. Obviously they will en-joy all the amenities of a town: schools and kindergartens, churches, shops, bank branches and cinemas. But the inner city now often lacks the vitality that has dissipated in having been removed to the satellite areas. In the evening when the offices and department stores have closed and everyone heads home to his residential new town, the heart of the city is disquieteningly empty. Then the roles are switched – the inner city becomes the satellite of the satellite town, even dependent on it – at least until morning when the routine is played out again.

The Old and the New: Wuppertal-Vohwinkel in North Rhine-Westphalia

Frankfurt: shopping centre in the north-west of town

Frankfurt: condominium block of flats on the Main quay

The New Shopping Centres

The more distant the new residential developments are located from the inner city, the more urgently shopping facilities are required. Everything needed for day-to-day life has to be available for "hauling in" – as the Berliners say – right on the spot. For this reason the grocery supermarkets have been planned accordingly. These new shops, based on a new marketing psychology, take up a great deal of space and they get it. But it is far different from that in the narrow inner city with their strolling areas. As the great demise of the cinema houses began, these picture palaces were largely converted into supermarkets. But once this opportunity had ceased to be, the supermarkets and all the goods they meanwhile had come to carry removed to the outskirts. This step was made possible because almost everyone had a car, and motorized shopping became popular. They could guarantee ample parking space. Combining the necessary with the useful – and most profitable – shopping centres often of mammoth proportions went up adjacent to the residential developments. Nothing has been stinted to make for the comfort and convenience of the shopping visitor – beginning with a child-care centre, so that there is no item or service that is not available – from a car wash to a pre-fab house. Consumer delight in modern German society has risen to the dimensions of a great feast.

Berlin: the Congress Hall in the Tiergarten district; built in 1957 and designed by Hugh Stubbins; financed by a grant of the Benjamin Franklin Foundation

Berlin: the New Philharmonic; completed in 1963, it is a later work of Hans Scharoun.

New Moods in Architecture

Even if we presume that the cave was man's primeval housing, the basics of architecture have changed but little over the millennia – for what does our housing still consist of but caves of brick and mortar with doors and windows cut into them? This is also true for the great prestigious buildings, for castles and palaces, town halls, churches and theatres. The size of the concavity may be measured in terms of cubic feet per room as with residential buildings. What is different is that these concavities are exposed on the exterior and no longer hidden underground: they are meant to be seen; what is more – they should reveal their function. Climate, building materials, technology and our aethetic sensibilities all play a part in their coming into being and this we term architectural style. The style prevailing in our day will not get its name until generations later, once enough distance in time has been achieved. We contemporaries only have provisional terms for it. Whatever we may call the present-day style, we can hardly get around the word *concrete.* This new building material, in conjunction with reinforcing iron, with frames of steel and with glass in enormous panes initially seemed only fitting for no-nonsense functional buildings. Office and residential high-rises ranged upwards and upwards in our cities. That they are like cubes or cigar boxes is the token of their cool sobriety.

Düsseldorf: the new St. Matthew's Church in the borough of Garath; architect: Prof. Böhm

The fact that it is also possible to make dreams out of concrete, steel and glass was the subject of much talk and speculation – although this architecture of dreams was already down on paper long before combining the use of these new material was even practicable. Among the pioneers of this new architectural mood were Walter Gropius of the Bauhaus school; Otto Bartning, known for his churches; Bruno Taut, renowned for his domestic architecture; Erich Mendelsohn, famed for his industrial designs; and Mies van der Rohe, noted for his fair and exhibition planning. Among the dreamers we need but cite Hans Poelzig, who remodelled Berlin's Grosses Schauspielhaus into a stalactite cave and Hans Scharoun, whose new building to accomodate the Berlin Philharmonic is probably the best-known example of an architectural dream come true. This structure develops entirely from its interior outwards, completely consonant with its function as a concert hall, a house of sound. But this does not mean that no consideration was made of how it would look on the outside. One will look in vain for the conventional façade, because as a concavity it dips down in easy sequence on the exterior to bring the entrance into focus – yet not arbitrarily, but as if ordained by the same spirit that also ordered the vaulted integrity of the interior.

Theatre: The Germans' Favorite Toy

The theatre – it is the most beloved plaything the Germans know. The fewest of the few play in that they do the acting, but the great majority play by being the audience. Yet all partake of its pleasures, this in a country, the social upheavals of which in recent times have all but vitiated its society both as a concept and an actuality; this notwithstanding, the society of the theatre has survived, the society of its public.

This is no coincidence. The tragic conflict of the passions and the wanton consternations of love will furnish the eternal stuff of the prose of all nations. But for the Germans they must first be dramatized before they can be taken seriously. This is why Schiller is the playwright closest to the people, because his was the inclination to convert everything into theatrical terms; even his most famous poem, *The Song of the Bell* – every schoolchild knows it – is basically the drama of life writ short. And as often as this poem is declaimed, theatre is performed with the same frequency, even if before no audience but its own. The German addiction to theatre cannot be explained in rational terms. If this predilection were the privilege of the few, it would be easier for the outside observer; but the love of theatre criss-crosses every age group, ethnic strain, station in life and annual income. This general trait in the German character is elucidated by the astonishing fact that German taxpayers come up with incomparably higher sums for their theatres than do those in any other nation – and this without a murmur of complaint. Now if a taxpayer does not get his dander up about this, it means he must have some peculiar thing about him; this attitude can thus have only one interpretation: his heart is in it. Only this explains the singular procedure unique in all the world that sees hundreds of people filing into hundreds of theatres evening after evening who fall into a hush when the chamber darkens and who then lapse into the enchantment of another world. In cold-nosed business terms, these are people with season tickets to whom, if the truth must be known, it matters not a bit to which work of art or kind of entertainment they have been gathered. They go to the theatre, they compose their thoughts or let them stray, in the intervals stroll to and fro – and suddenly in half-hours such as these Germany has formed a society, a theatre society in the foyers. And this does not merely mean tossing back dry martinis and raving about exciting scenes; it is a true empathizing with a new play, some new music, a new production. The prickly sensation of being on the spot, as with any other society, is enhanced by the splendour of the surroundings, aye, the splendour of having appeared there oneself.

Darmstadt: the new Staatstheater, completed in 1972; architect: Rolf Prange; foreground: spheres by the Italian sculptor Arnaldo Pomodoro

Düsseldorf: Neues Schauspielhaus, completed in 1969; architect: Bernhard Pfau

Administration building of the nuclear power station at Stade; it was put into service in 1972.

The Beauty of New Functional Buildings

The concavity descending on the exterior reminds us, not by chance, of the tent, the second primeval form of human dwellings. Hans Scharoun, in speaking of his design for the Berlin Philharmonic, has stated: "In terms of form it has the effect of a tent. This tent-like contour means it is convex and lies in close conjunction with acoustics in an attempt to spread the music as diffusely as possible within the chamber." The architects of contemporary churches arrived at the tent form via a completed different route; they took the Biblical term "the Lord's tent" in its literal sense and in so doing justified their retreat from church interiors of the past; their altars could thus no longer appear as the continuation of the longitudinal axis because there is no longer such an axis nor the easily discernible basic outline. Now the altar stands in the centre of the congregation in the tent. By the same token, the builders of the great exhibition halls or mammoth sports facilities arrived at t model of the tent for utterly different considerations. The tent's original purpose of offering protection from wind, weather or attack after centuries of experience with it has led to structures now available for the use of all, once rigid stone could be dispensed with. The tent roofing for the athletic facilities at the Olympic Games in Munich represent the finest example of this. They combine the light – even provisional-looking – element of the tents, although built to last, with the contours of the surrounding land to form a new type of beauty that traces its origin back to the oldest form of functionalism.

Olympic grounds at Munich: tent structure at the main entrance

Protected as National Monuments?

Industrial buildings represent the purest form of functional architecture that can possibly be imagined. Thus the winding tower of a coal mine fulfils its purpose and nothing else. It would never occur to anyone to behold it as an aspect of beauty. Yet the number of instances is increasing in which industrial buildings are also being placed under protection as national monuments in Germany. They are intended to be preserved for their artistic value or significance in cultural history. Castles and palaces are followed by factory buildings or tram repair shops. Can they not be said to follow them with equal justification?

Anthracite coal mine, 3,280 feet underground, at the "Hans Aden" mine near Oberaden, north of Dortmund; coal planer with conveyor belt and hydraulic pistons in the seam

Six-thousand-ton press at the Klöckner Works in Osnabrück

German Cars
All Over the World

Of all car-manufacturing nations in the world, Germany with her 16 makes out of a total of 100 occupies second place; she lies between the United States, with 29 makes and Japan with 14. But Germany takes first place as a car-exporting nation – no surprise to anyone abroad who is a car spotter. He will encounter them in the most remote corners of the earth and certainly in the most bustling. The Mercedes and Volkswagen makes have attained world-wide fame in this manner – the "Bug" because it happens along so unpretentiously, the Mercedes with its three-pointed star because of quite the opposite. The latter's pretensions are not without justification, because it descends in direct line from Carl Benz, the man who as early as 1886 had conceived a vehicle driven by a four-stroke engine. By contrast, the Volkswagen is an adventurer who broke into the aristocracy of the Ford, the Opel, the Renault and the Fiat. Ferdinand Porsche developed it in 1934. Used as a kind of jeep by the German Wehrmacht, it withstood the test of its mettle in the Second World War. Coming from Wolfsburg, the city it alone had turned into an economic miracle, it was the very embodiment of the German economic miracle and it conquered the world.

Canopied pedestrian passageway at the Düsseldorf fairgrounds

Fairs of International Rank

The much-touted economic miracle represents in fact nothing more than a virtue the Germans made of necessity. The devastated cities and factories were there while displaced persons and refugees fled into the country by the millions. It was not simply a matter of hard work and a talent for organization; each hour demanded some new type of improvisation as every day called for the gift of invention. The postwar period put Germany's vitality to the test. Even dismantling certain industries worked out to the good as far as that was concerned; the very newest machinery was moved into the vacant factory sheds – machines that could by far outclass all others in performance that still were in use all around Europe. Along with them came greater efficiency and automation – early on by a decisive number of years. This was in the air even at the first postwar German industrial fairs; the Hanover Fair was first held in 1946 and has since become an indispensable event. The old Frankfurt Spring Fair soon regained its former importance. In that city a new type of fair came into being – the book fair, a fair of the mind. International in character and held annually, it has grown to become the one great rendezvous of the publishers, sellers and purveyors of literature for all the world, a stock market of the intellect. Here best-sellers are made and authors dealt in, much like stocks and bonds.

Hanover Industrial Fair

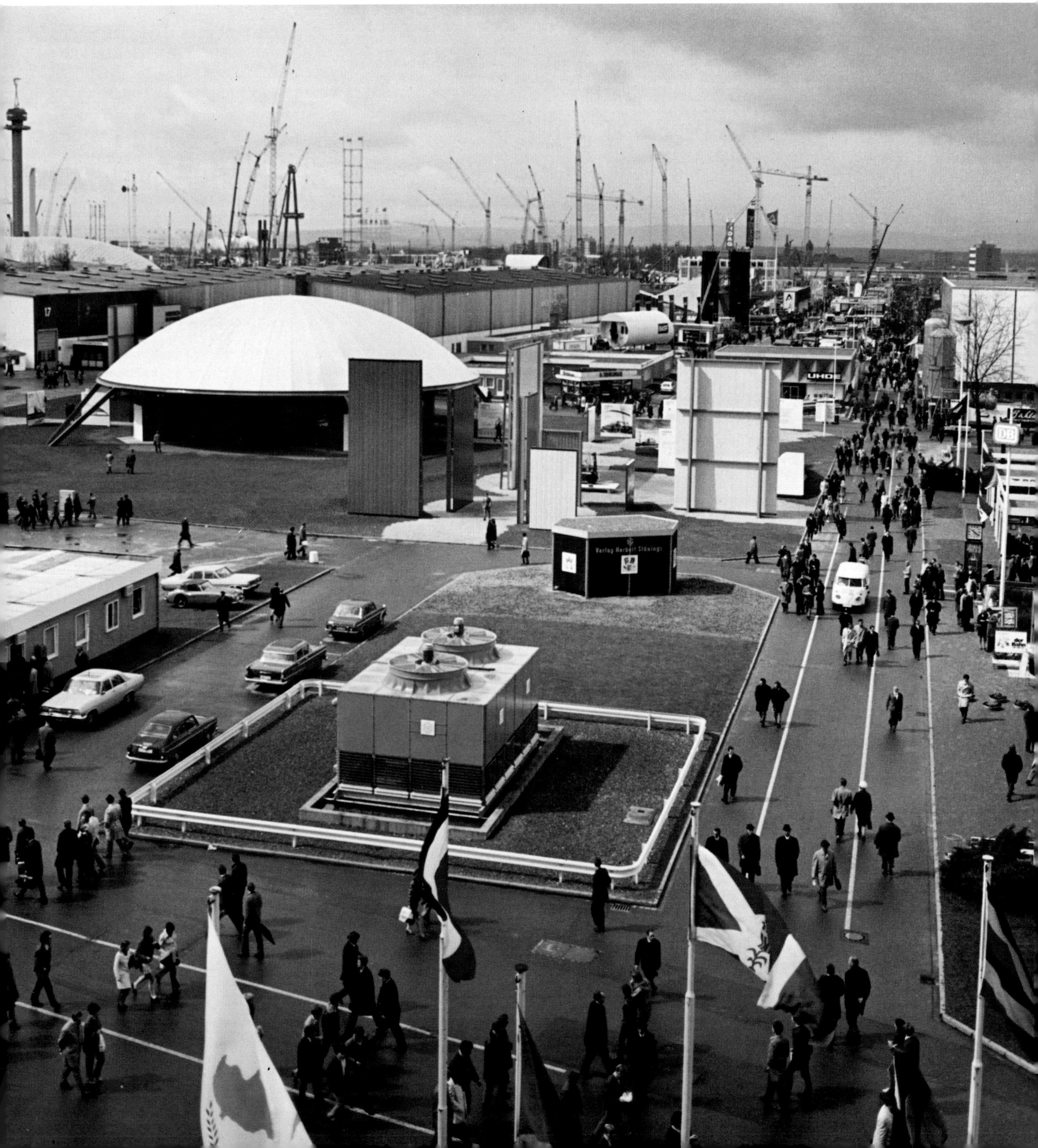

Markets — The Oldest Form of Trade

Each city in Germany has had its markets from the year dot – indeed, even smaller communities have developed by virtue of certain conditions into market towns with the status of borough. In ancient times the market was the place for the conduct of public life, and most especially for the exchange and sale of goods of every description. It has also been maintained in Germany as an indispensable fixture for centuries on end and often specialized for certain types of goods or commodities, such as a cattle, grain, hay or fish market. Today as back in the Middle Ages city people like to visit the weekly markets held with the intent of buying vegetables and other farm produce at better bargains because there the middleman has often been cut out. In any event, farmers like to seize this opportunity of cultivating immediate contacts with city people, and the city people for once have the advantage of getting truly fresh produce from the producer. These are among the economic advantages of the market. In addition, it offers a certain appeal that is lacking in the giant fairs and exhibitions with their massive attendance, for it is at the local market that housewives gladly yield to temptation. On market days they somehow find the municipal market with its colourful umbrellas and opulent selection of goods much nicer than elsewhere. They wander from stand to stand, look at what is on sale, compare prices, see familiar faces and have a chat. No department store ever so large nor any specialty shop ever so well stocked can offer such diversion. Without markets, Germany's towns would be much poorer

Central market in Trier; left rear: St. Gangolf's

Weekly market on the Schillerplatz in Stuttgart

A modern Intercity train

Bavaria's train up the Zugspitze

In a TEE observation car

Names of the Fast Trains

The first locomotive manufactured by Henschel at Kassel in 1848 was christened "The Dragon", as befitted a steam-huffing and puffing monster. But such imaginative names had to give way to reality as the railway became a fixture of everyday life, else they would ill suit the timetables. In their stead came numbers. Yet this has changed since the emergence of especially fast and comfortable passenger trains. Now they have names again and individuals have sprung from prosaic numbers. Today's Intercity trains travel from 33 German cities to 33 German cities – up to eight times per day, and direct connections may be made at any of five cities: Hanover, Dortmund, Cologne, Würzburg and Mannheim. A person can change trains on the same platform and the connecting train will arrive concurrently. This network is becoming denser and denser as additional routes and connecting routes for shorter runs are added. By their names these trains reveal where they started or where they are headed: the *Rheinpfeil,* or *Rhine Arrow* covers Munich, Duisburg and Hanover; the *Schwabenpfeil* or *Swabian Arrow,* Hamburg, Cologne and Stuttgart; the *Münchner Kindl,* (roughly: *Munich Child*) goes from Munich to Cologne and then east to Hanover; the *Toller (mad) Bomberg* connects Hamburg with Duisburg. The TEEs, or Trans-European Express trains have taken names that set them apart. The one that travels daily from Frankfurt to Paris and return is named after a son of Frankfurt who never once in his life ever got to Paris; it is called *Goethe.* A *Parcival* goes via Aachen to Hamburg and we may journey from Zürich or Basle to Hamburg on the *Helvetia,* or from Milan via Basle to Bremen on the *Roland.*

The Autobahn — and All It Implies

The 3,230 miles of the German Autobahn system are taken for granted by the motorist. Ever now and then he might take slight notice once a new section or connecting route representing those additional thousand miles that have been under construction all this time are finally opened up to traffic. That seems only right and proper as far as he is concerned, even though he bears his share in financing them in higher fuel prices or other means of taxation. The longer the distances get to be, the more urgently he needs stopping places, filling stations and refreshment stops. As soon as the motorist becomes a motorized tourist, he requires all the amenities a tourist wants. It so happens that a "Society of Ancillary Services for the Federal Autobahn" sees to such things. It does not operate on public funds but is financed by the capital services market. Of the 170 "rest stations" it operates, 48 have a connecting motel, which taken together offer 2,700 beds. It has restaurants with waiter service and cafeterias and combinations of the two. In addition, at every second of the 230 filling stations light refreshments are available. Also, anyone not patronizing the restaurants to eat may use the telephone, wash up, or even take advantage of the children's playgrounds. More than a hundred rest stops offer their own baby-changing rooms. The menus range from a light snack for the driver to rich stews to the culinary specialities of the region – best left to those not in the driver's seat.

The Walldorf Autobahn cloverleaf between Heidelberg and Karlsruhe (air-photo courtesy government of Swabia, No. 5/5113)

Haseltal Autobahn bridge in the Spessart forest near Frankfurt

In the International Airway System

Thanks to its geographical location Frankfurt has grown to boast Europe's third-largest airport – after London's Heathrow and Paris' Orly. At peak travel hours it must be prepared to handle up to forty take-offs and landings per hour. A new enlarged facility had to be built, included longer runways. After being ten years under construction Frankfurt's new airport was opened in March 1972 – on proportions adequate for the traffic expected by 1980 – 30 million passengers per year as opposed to today's ten million. Apart from scheduled passenger traffic, charter flights and air freight are ever on the increase. It was not misplanned – it was just the fact that the new terminus of three gargantuan halls under one roof came across as a labyrinth calculated to frighten the wits out of any passenger. But after a year had passed it got into stride. Frankfurt is on the way to having the "nicest airport in the world".

≪The new airport at Rhine-Main (air-photo courtesy president of government in Darmstadt, No. 872/72)

Below: Passenger Terminal at Rhine-Main Airport

Arriving Passengers' Building at Rhine-Main Airport

Water Routes and Seaports

On the Rhine, Europe's most heavily travelled water route, it is only proper that Europe's largest inland harbour of Duisburg should be located. With its twenty berths to meet the cargo traffic, it even exceeds many a large seaport. It trades in bulk goods such as sand and gravel, iron and scrap metal, fertilizers, salts, grain and coal. The network of canals between the Ruhr and the Weser belongs to the Rhine, as well as connections to the seaports of Bremen and Emden. Still under construction is the Rhine-Main-Danube Canal, which will connect the North Sea with the Black Sea as one major water route.

The German seaports – Emden, Wilhelmshaven, Bremen and Bremerhaven, Hamburg and Lübeck are all in the liveliest of competition with Rotterdam, Amsterdam and Antwerp. This means they must maintain the most modern transshipment facilities. The German merchant fleet is no less up-to-date; the average age of the ships is nine years. But it is also small in proportion to the growth in Germany's sea-borne foreign trade. The German tanker fleet is particularly disproportionally small to the constantly increasing demand for oil from the Middle East and overseas.

Shipping on the Lower Rhine

Duisburg: Germany's largest inland shipping harbour

In Hamburg Harbour (p. 224)
Loading tobacco bales in Bremerhaven (p. 225)

The Okertal dam in the Harz, near Altenau

Water — A Quality of Life

As both air and water began to become polluted before our very
eyes – a product of civilization not confined to any one country –
the watchword came into use: "the quality of life". What did people
wish to gain back? Nothing else but what even a half a century ago
was taken as a matter of course. Pure air and clean water have risen
to be regarded as qualities of life. The Federal Republic has enough
water; it is merely a question of how it will be able to restore polluted
water into the natural cycle and how it can coexist economically with
the available ground water supply. These concerns had their incep-
tion with supplying water to the large cities of the Ruhr district; they
were alleviated by building dams and this killed a number of birds
with one stone, among them regulating the water level of the rivers,
generating electricity and improving the climate. But since this pre-
scription is not universally practicable, other means have to be devised. Interconnecting systems have thus come into being for distri-
buting the precious supply and these independent of international
borders. In addition, attempts are being made to use the water in a
circulatory process and this entails constructing biological and chemical purification stages or filtering stations. Since the portion of
high-quality and economically accessible ground water and spring
water of the total supply available lowers from year to year, this is
regarded as the sole solution.

Water purification plant in Düsseldorf-Hamm on the Rhine

Oil – A Problem of Energy

The world is starving for oil and Germany shares in the appetite for this form of energy that runs its cars and heats its residences. Millions of tons of crude oil are fed into the Federal Republic by pipeline. From the Mediterranean ports of Marseille, Genoa and Trieste these pipelines go via France to Karlsruhe to the refineries, over via Italy and Austria to Ingolstadt. The refineries near Cologne are connected direct with the harbours of Rotterdam and Wilhelmshaven.

Major refinery in Rüsselsheim-Raunheim: CALTEX petroleum plant

Pipeline construction in the Siebengebirge

Construction fence as a canvas for up-and-coming artists

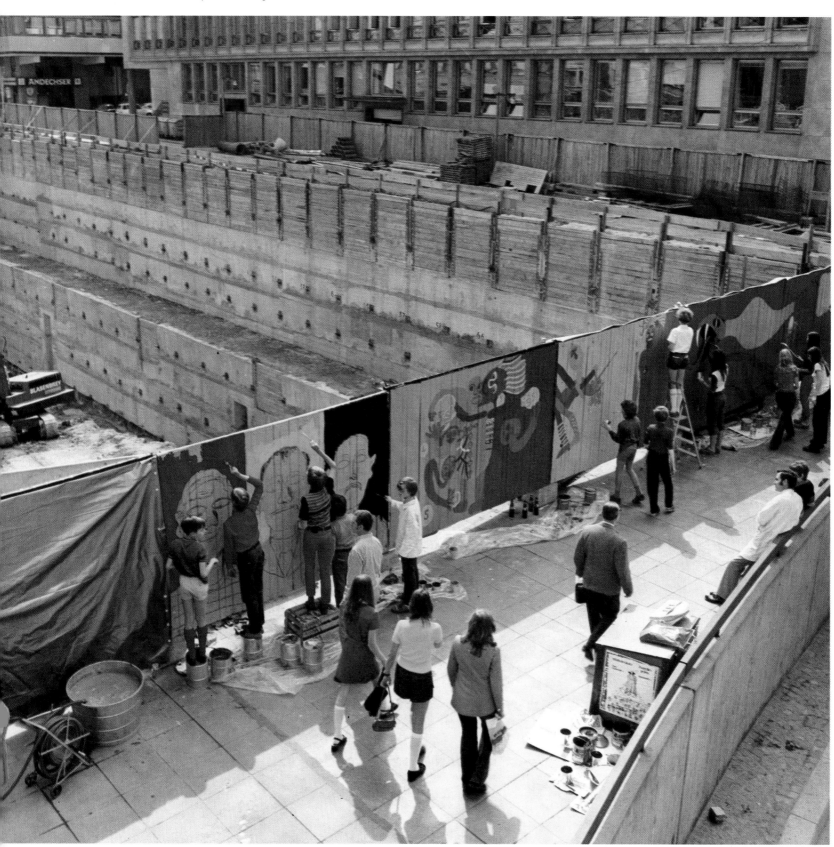

Learning by Playing

Our future is our youth. But the guidelines of how that future will appear in detail is in increasing degree no longer determined by pedagogues of an older mentality but those with newer approaches. For these teachers the education of children offers the earliest opportunity of warding off "authoritarian structures". A great variety of patterns exist for the new approaches to education. They all are concerned with the child even at the pre-school age. And all of them at least are in agreement that children should not be taught "on orders" but by playing. They are encouraged to make up stories or tell them; they are given paper, brush and colours without prescribing the outcome. Forces are unleashed by relying on the child's imagination.

Young reader's staircase
in the Stuttgart municipal library

Modern Schools and Universities

Between 1960 and 1970 thirteen new institutes of higher learning were founded in the Federal Republic, of which ten were of university status. Otherwise the explosion in student enrolments could no longer be kept under control. The fact that these new universities – a good example is the Ruhr University of Bochum – also entail a new concept of education – known as the "total university" – will be obvious. Since a total university will no longer be rigidly divided into the various disciplines, it is easier for a student to phase over from one direction of study to another than is possible in the university of the conventional type.

Reforming primary and secondary eductation and schools of further education is proceeding parallel with the reform of the system of advanced education. The vertical system of the school system of the past is being discarded; in its place the "total school" is expected to be established, in which – as in the total university – it will be easier for pupils in schools to enjoy the opportunity of changing the emphasis of their schooling to different subjects.

Humboldt Gymnasium in Neuss

The new Ruhr University of Bochum

The Advancement of Science

The German Research Association is concerned with the advancement of scientific research. Its membership includes all institutes of higher learning belonging to the West German Conference of University Chancellors, the academies of science, the Max Planck Society, the German Association of Technological and Scientific Societies. the Society of German Natural Science Researchers and Physicians, the Federal Institute of Physics and Technology and the Fraunhofer Society for the Advancement of the Sciences. It is financed by the Federal government, by the constituent states of West Germany and – via the Donors Association for German Science – by the private sector. The Max Planck Society for the Advancement of the Sciences primarily enables those men of learning who have dedicated themselves to basic research the opportunity to conduct scientific work without impediment. At present it supports fifty research institutes. The scientific achievements it can claim have won extraordinary acclaim both at home and abroad. The directors of its institutes are in great measure scientists with international reputations. Several of them are Nobel Prize laureates. Eighty per cent of the support for the Max Planck Society comes from public sources and 20% from donations, including the contributions of the Donors Association and the Volkswagen Foundation. The Donors Association for German Science is a group formed from the sectors of private industry and the professions. Its sole and exclusive purpose is to advance scientific research, teaching and training. It gathers donations and passes them on for this purpose. Thus more than half of the donations received are applied to the German Research Association. In addition, the scientific academies, the Max Planck Society, the German Academic Exchange Service, the Alexander von Humboldt Foundation and the Studies Foundation of the German People are all subvented by funds from every source. Between 1949 and 1966 the Donors Association was able to raise 300 million marks.

(Portions of the above have been cited from *Tatsachen über Deutschland,* published by the Press and Information Office of the Federal government.)

Electronic microscope at the Siemens Works in Berlin▷

The nuclear reactor at Jülich (p. 236)
100-metre radio telescope at Effelsberg in the Eifel mountains (p. 237)

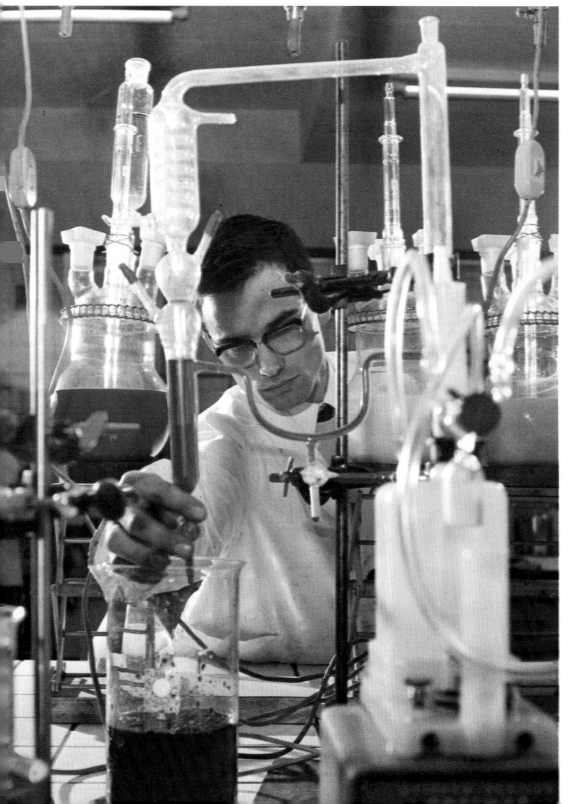

Laboratory of a chemical works

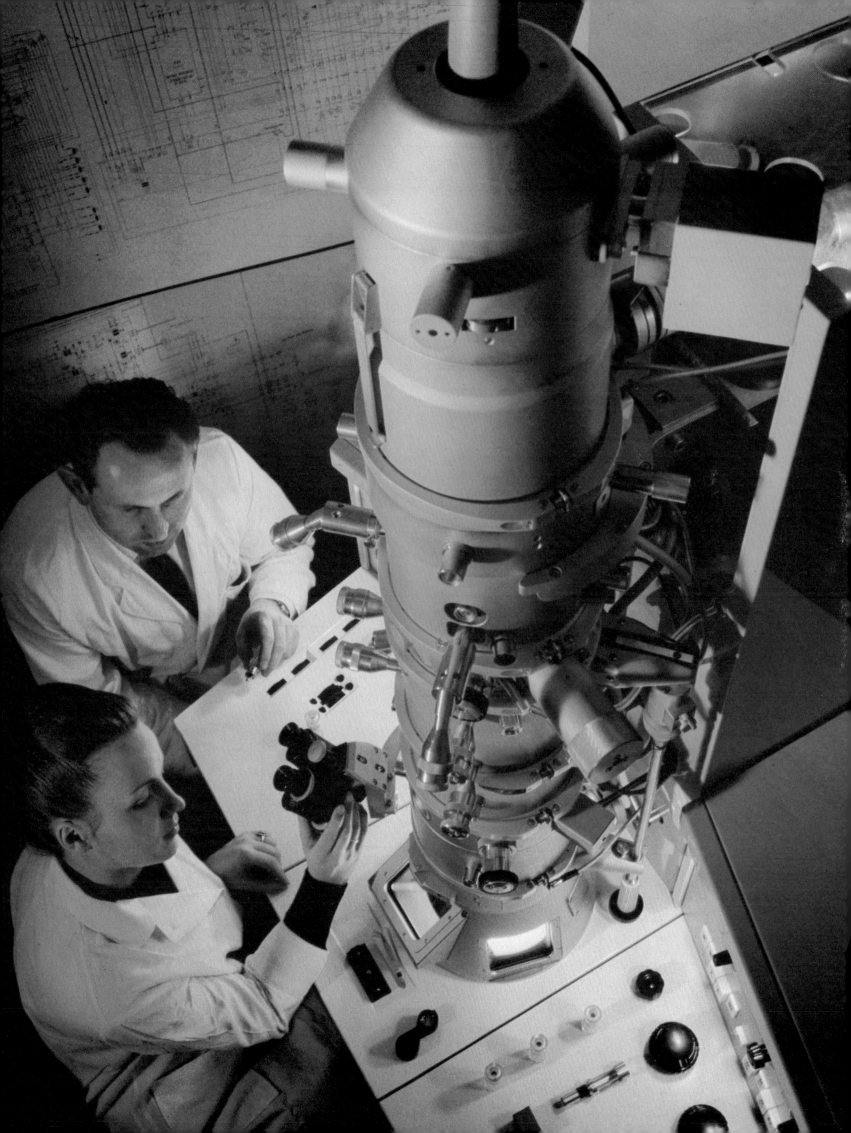

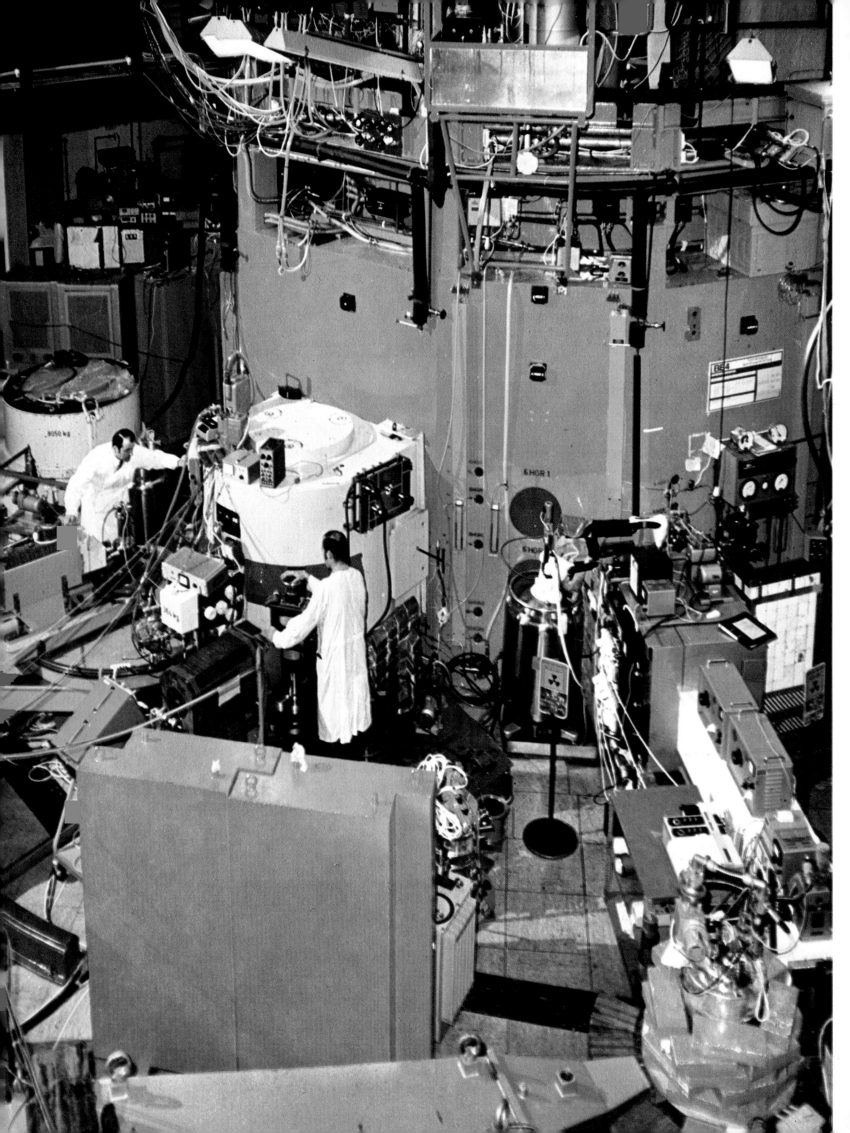

Islands of Green and Garden Plots

The order of a Berlin tavern keeper to his servant: "Gottlieb, take the garden outdoors!" – meaning two puny oleander sprouts in a bucket such as might be found on the first sunny day of spring – is a favourite old joke. It is indicative of the big city dweller's yearning for "mother green". Berliners call the tiny strip of land where they can

Island of green in the Ruhr district

puttering around on their own their "arbour". There with his whole family he will spend every free minute of the warm season. And there is practically no large German city that does not also have its "arbours". These are known as "Schreber gardens", falsely attributed to a Leipzig physician of the same name who lived from 1808 to 1861 and who undoubtedly did his bit for the promotion of public health. The fact remains he had nothing to do with the idea of small garden plots. Their actual "inventor" was a school principal named Hauschild, who a hundred years ago propagated the idea of small garden colonies as farms in miniature.

In a Berlin Schreber garden

Race on the Nürburgring

240

Spectator sport: football fans

The Finest Diversion in the World

"King Football" also reigns in Germany; the public's interest in this sport is all-surpassing. For this reason the German Football League has more members than any other sports association. But right on its heels is the German Gymnastics League. Somewhat farther behind are the German Rifle Association and German Light Athletics Association. This list may indicate something of the order of preferences, but it does not take non-organized sports into account, not the likes of swimmers or skiers or hikers that pursue their sport outside any organized club or league. Sports are obligatory in all schools. All young people in school participate in the "Federal Youth Games". What is more, the State encourages sports, but does not exercise any manner of compulsion for the public to "keep fit". Sports are a private matter, yet as it has been noted they are the "finest diversion in the world."

Carrier Pigeon Buffs

Owners of carrier pigeons in Germany – and their association boasts almost a hundred thousand members – are located overwhelmingly in the Ruhr district, and this for good reason. Miners toiling beneath the earth see in the pigeon the very embodiment of life out in the light. A miner can send his longings off on a trip. Neither pigeon nor these longings just flutter away off in the blue; they always return. A pigeon's innate sense of location and their speed in flight can be improved through breeding. The sporting element of competition enhances the pleasure. Bets are made and carrier pigeons get to be the "racing horses of the little man". As far as yearnings are concerned, the breeders' "travel associations" reflect these longings in such names as "Over Land and Sea", or "Come Back Again".

Old Swabian winehouse

Knights of "Gemütlichkeit"

The German word "Gemüt" is untranslatable; foreigners have sought to define it "as the seat of inner sensibilities". Germans consider "Gemüt" as a third force between heart and spirit. But what is utterly untranslatable is the word derived from it: "Gemütlichkeit". It betokens less of an inner feeling than an outer state of a feeling of well-being. It may be encountered in the family living room where Christmas is celebrated as the red-letter feast of "Gemütlichkeit", but outside the family circle as well in the neighbourhood tavern where a person will have his *Stammtisch* – a table the proprietor reserves for favoured patrons and friends. There he may play at *Skat* or *Schafskopf* or simply chat about the news of his village or town or his local district of the city over a glass of beer. In the South-West the beverage will more likely be a *Viertele* or quarter-litre of wine. But "Gemütlichkeit" is not just for men; the women's "Kaffeeklatsch" has its own chummy atmosphere that is so easily invoked in Germany but so hard to comprehend abroad. "Where or when, 'tis a noble sight/To behold the knights of "Gemütlichkeit . . .", runs an old song; it has been sung a hundred years and will still be sung for many yet to come.

The German national card game: *Skat*

Jazz concert in Bad Cannstatt's pleasure gardens

At the Dahlem Museum in Berlin: Rembrandt's "Man with a Golden Helmet"

In the Museum

People are headed back to the museum; the number of visitors increasing uninterruptedly over the years is proof of this. This is not simply due to the "open-door policy" now followed by German museums; it is also a function of seeing them in the original face-to-face that is only possible in a museum. The better known a work of art is through reproductions or replicas, the more urgent the desire will be to see it in the original. Of the Federal Republic's approximately 1300 museums and museums of local history and culture, art museums and historical collections take first place; they have their base in such old seats of government as Munich, Stuttgart, Karlsruhe, Darmstadt, Kassel, Hanover, Brunswick and, of course, Berlin. Famous as the gathering place of older German and European art are the "Pinakotheken" and Bavarian National Museum in Munich, the Germanic National Museum in Nuremberg, the State Galeries in Stuttgart and Karlsruhe the Städelian Institute of Art in Frankfurt, the Painting Gallery in Kassel, the Duke Anton-Ulrich Museum in Brunswick, the museums at Hamburg and Bremen, the Wallraf-Richartz Museum, and the Schnütgen Museum in Cologne. The German Museum in Munich exhibits the masterpieces of science and technology, these as wittnesses to progress.

811A REMBRANDT HARMENSZ VAN RIJN 1606-1669 DER MANN MIT DEM GOLDHELM
EIGENTUM DES KAISER-FRIEDRICH-MUSEUMS-VEREINS

A performance in the Schiller-Theater in Berlin

The Great Masters

As readily as the Germans acknowledge the federal structure of its Republic and its constituent states such as Bavaria, Hesse or Lower Saxony, the less willingly would they speak of a particular Bavarian, Hessian or Lower Saxon culture. The fact is that no one speaks in such terms as in all truth it would never occur to a German to term Dürer a Bavarian, Goethe as a Hessian, Schiller as a Württemberger or Beethoven as a Rhinelander. These men have all suceeded in capturing the very quintessence of what we know as German culture. It is rooted in all German strains and races and – to follows the simile of a tree – its foliage spreads over the entire nation.

An oratorio in St. Michael's Church, Hamburg

A Country's New Countenance

By the summer of 1972 the time had come: the Federal Republic of Germany should and could pass out its calling card. It did so by holding the Summer Olympic Games once it had gained this privilege after a lapse of 38 years. In contrast to the previous event when a Reich wanted to show itself off and let its military might awaken dread fear, the 1972 Games showed the happy and peaceful country of "Swinging Germany". Anyone who saw the procession of the nations on the jubilant opening day, whether on the spot in Munich or at home by the television set can be called an eye witness to this basic transformation. The black shadow of an act of terrorism that cast itself precipitously over the Games did in sum total dampen the joy of the initial success. Nevertheless, the world, as it were, was given the opportunity of observing German society as a living corporate body – and not in the abstrac as often the contrived show-window nature of many an international exposition as at Brussels, Montreal or Tokyo. In Munich, Augsburg, Kiel or wherever the Olympic competitions were held, reality had to speak for the country, the reality of everday German life. In this manner it is felt that the march-past of the nations in Munich bears its analogy in the utterly unceremonious entry of the new image of present-day Germany into the consciousness of all peoples of the world.

The Olympic Games in Munich, 1972: the opening ceremonies

Germany at the international
exhibition in Osaka, Japan, in 1970

The German Pavilion
at Expo '67 in Montreal

State visit of Queen Juliana
of The Netherlands to Bonn in 1972

Our Pictures

A to Z

in this volume contain place names, mountains, lakes and river scenes